THOMAS COOK
Travellers

TURKEY

BY
DIANA DARKE

AA

Produced by AA Publishing

Written by Diana Darke

Original photography by Dario Mitidieri

Edited, designed and produced by AA
Publishing. Maps © The Automobile Association 1994

Distributed in the United Kingdom by AA Publishing,
Fanum House, Basingstoke, Hampshire, RG21 2EA.

The contents of this publication are believed correct at the
time of printing. Nevertheless, the publishers cannot be held
responsible for any errors or omissions or for changes in the
details given in this guide or for the consequences of any
reliance on the information provided by the same.
Assessments of attractions, hotels, restaurants and so forth
are based upon the author's own experience and, therefore,
descriptions given in this guide necessarily contain an element
of subjective opinion which may not reflect the publishers' opinion or
dictate a reader's own experiences on another occasion.
**We have tried to ensure accuracy in this guide, but things do
change and we would be grateful if readers would advise us of
any inaccuracies they may encounter.**

A CIP catalogue record for this book is available from the British
Library.

ISBN 0 7495 0698 9

Published by AA Publishing (a trading name of Automobile Association
Developments Limited, whose registered office is Fanum House,
Basingstoke, Hampshire RG21 2EA. Registered number 1878835) and
the Thomas Cook Group Ltd.

Colour separation: BTB Colour Reproduction, Whitchurch, Hampshire

Printed by Edicoes ASA, Oporto, Portugal

Cover picture: *The Blue Mosque, Istanbul*
Title page: *Reading the Koran in a Diyarbakir mosque*
Above: *Temple of Apollo at Side*

Contents

About this Book

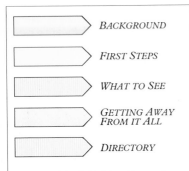

BACKGROUND

FIRST STEPS

WHAT TO SEE

GETTING AWAY FROM IT ALL

DIRECTORY

This book is divided into five sections, identified by the above colour coding.

The **Background** gives an introduction to the country – its history, geography, politics, culture.

First Steps offers practical advice on arriving and getting around.

What to See is an alphabetical listing of places to visit, divided into seven regions, interspersed with walks and tours.

Getting Away From it All highlights places off the beaten track where it's possible to relax and enjoy peace and quiet.

Finally, the **Directory** provides practical information – from shopping and entertainment to children and sport, including a section on business matters. Special highly illustrated features on specific aspects of the country appear throughout the book.

Antalya yacht harbour

BACKGROUND

'The Turk is unusually full of contradictions. Not only has he East and West in him, European and Asian, but an intense pride combined with an acute inferiority complex, a deep xenophobia with an overwhelming hospitality to strangers, a profound need for flattery with an absolute disregard for what anybody thinks of him.'

DAVID HOTHAM,
Times correspondent (1975)

Introduction

*T*urkey is a remarkable passage-land between Europe and Asia, and the country reflects these two identities. The western half, with the cities of Istanbul, Izmir and Antalya, is richer and more densely populated, looking towards Europe and the Mediterranean. The other part, from Ankara eastwards, with its rugged, haunting steppelands of Anatolia, points more towards Turkey's Asian heritage.

It is to the western part that most visitors come, drawn by the legendary magic of Istanbul and by the longest and cleanest coastline in the Mediterranean. Eastern Turkey remains a different story, more suited to the adventurer than the beach-lover.

Perhaps the most surprising

discoveries for first-time visitors are the excellent food and drink at affordable prices, and the dignity of the Turkish people. In terms of ancient remains, both western and eastern Turkey offer a wealth verging on superfluity, with archaeological sites reaching back to the Stone Age and the Hittites, through

TURKEY

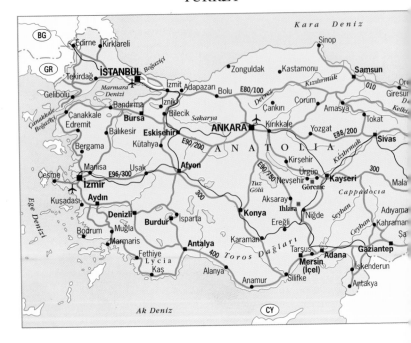

Greek and Roman cities, to Byzantine, Seljuk and Ottoman monuments. Many are in magnificent settings. Natural wonders are everywhere – caves, waterfalls, canyons, volcanoes, lakes and

The turquoise waters of Ölü Deniz near Fethiye

springs, with some of the most stunning mountain scenery in the world.

THOMAS COOK'S TURKEY

Visits to Turkey by Thomas Cook tourists began soon after he had established his Egyptian business in 1869. By 1877 Constantinople (Istanbul) had become an essential part of a Middle East tour and Cook passengers on the Orient Express were soon added to those who embarked here for Alexandria. Further tours were added as the Wagons-Lits Company extended its services to Smyrna (Izmir). By 1913 Thomas Cook was advertising such exotic tours as Mount Ararat by rail. In more recent times Thomas Cook have promoted holidays at Turkish seaside resorts, city breaks to Istanbul and gület cruises.

History

7500BC
First Stone Age settlements at
Çatalhüyük.

1900–1300BC
Hittite Empire with Hattuşaş
(Boğazkale) as capital, contemporary
with ancient Egypt and Babylon.

1250BC
The Trojan War. Fall of Troy (Truva).

1200–700BC
Migration of Greeks to Aegean coastal
regions. Kingdoms of Phrygia, Ionia,
Lycia, Lydia, Caria and Pamphylia.
Urartian civilisation in eastern Anatolia.

700BC
Birth of Homer in Smyrna (Izmir).
Beginnings of Hellenistic culture in
Aegean Turkey.

546BC
Cyrus the Great of Persia invades.
Anatolia under Persian rule.

334BC
Alexander the Great conquers Anatolia,
freeing it from the Persians.

130BC
Anatolia becomes the Roman province of
Asia with capital at Ephesus (Efes).

40BC
Antony and Cleopatra marry at Antioch.

AD47–57
St Paul's missionary journeys. First
Christian community at Antioch.

AD313
Christianity accepted as official religion
by the Roman Empire.

AD330
Byzantium renamed Constantinople by
Emperor Constantine as new capital of
Byzantine Empire.

527–565
Reign of Justinian and the height of
Byzantine power.

636–718
Muslim Arabs defeat Byzantines and
besiege Constantinople.

1054
Schism between Greek and Roman
churches.

1071–1243
Seljuk Turks conquer Anatolia with
Konya as their capital.

1096–1204
The Crusades, with Latin armies
entering Anatolia for the first time.
Byzantine Empire dismembered.

1288
Birth of Ottoman Empire with capital at
Bursa.

1453
Mehmet II conquers Constantinople and
renames it Istanbul as capital of
Ottoman Empire.

1520–1566
Reign of Süleyman the Magnificent and
the Golden Age of the Ottoman Empire,
which extended from the Danube to
Aden and Eritrea, and from the
Euphrates and the Crimea to Algiers.

1682–1725
Reign of Peter the Great in Russia begins
new phase of Russo-Turkish rivalry.

1854
Crimean War. Ottomans are supported
by British and French against Russia.

1909
Abdul Hamid, last Ottoman sultan,
deposed by Young Turks.

1914
Turkey enters World War I as ally of
Germany. On defeat, the Allies propose
carve-up of Ottoman Empire.

1915
Gallipoli Campaign. Allied landings on
Turkish soil are repulsed.

1919

Atatürk leads Turkish resistance in fight for national sovereignty.

1923

Turkish state proclaimed with Atatürk as President. Exchange of minority populations between Greece and Turkey. Reforms to modernise and secularise the state. Islam disestablished, Arabic script replaced by Latin alphabet, Turkish language revived. Women's veils and the fez banned.

1938

Atatürk dies.

1945

Turkey remains neutral in World War II.

1946

Turkey becomes charter member of United Nations.

1952

Turkey joins NATO.

1960

Almost bloodless military coup followed by successive inefficient governments.

1964

Turkey becomes associate member of the EEC.

1974

Turkey intervenes in Cyprus to protect the Turkish Cypriot community, seizing the northern third of the island.

1980

Bloodless military coup under General Kenan Evren, three years of military rule.

1983

Return to civilian rule with Turgut Özal elected Prime Minister, moving to the Presidency in 1989.

1985–1990

Disputes with Greece over Cyprus and Aegean territorial waters damage Turkey's attempts to join the EEC, as does its human rights record in handling Kurdish insurrection in the southeast.

Obelisk base, Istanbul Hippodrome

1991–1993

Süleyman Demirel elected Prime Minister forming a coalition government. Forms post of Minister for Human Rights and promises review of Kurdish policy. Economic reforms introduced to combat 70 per cent inflation.

1993

President Turgut Özal dies. Prime Minister Süleyman Demirel becomes his successor and Tansu Çiller becomes, in turn, the first woman Prime Minister.

NAME CHANGES

The name 'Anatolia', meaning the Asiatic part of modern Turkey, the Asian heartland, comes from the Greek word for east. Under the Romans this area was referred to as Asia Minor.

The city of Istanbul was originally called Byzantium when it was founded in 667BC, then renamed Constantinople by the Byzantines, before being renamed Istanbul by the Ottomans.

THE OTTOMAN EMPIRE
1326–1922

The Ottomans began as a small tribe of nomadic Turks and ended up as the power that overthrew the Byzantine Empire, dominating the region for the next 600 years. The name Ottoman, Turkish *Osmanlı*, is derived from their first leader Osman Gazi.

Their first capital was at Bursa in 1326, but their expansion suffered a severe setback when the Mongols under Tamerlane invaded from Central Asia in 1402. They recovered, and by 1453, under Sultan Mehmet II, they took Constantinople after a seven-week siege. Mehmet, thereafter called the Conqueror, began repairing the siege damage, and by 1470 had built the Topkapı Sarayı (Topkapı Palace) as the new imperial residence and completed the huge Fatih Camii, Mosque of the Conqueror, the first mosque complex of its kind. Mehmet also repopulated the city bringing in Turks, Greeks, Armenians and Spanish Jews. By the end of the 15th century, Istanbul, as the Turks now called it, was the thriving prosperous capital of an empire. Under Selim the Grim, the empire was extended to Persia, Syria and Egypt. He was preparing a great campaign against Europe when he died unexpectedly in 1520.

The Ottoman Empire reached its peak under Selim's son, Süleyman, known in the west as 'The Magnificent'. Vienna was his only military failure, saving Europe from further Ottoman expansion. He used the booty, tribute

Türbe of Süleyman the Magnificent, with the Süleymaniye mosque behind

Left: view from the Topkapı Palace
Below: Ottoman costumes c1825

and taxes from his conquered territories to adorn Istanbul with charitable institutions and mosque complexes, the grandest of which is the Süleymaniye.

The long slow decline of the Ottoman Empire started in 1566 with Süleyman's son, Selim II, known as 'The Sot'. Much of the decline is laid at the door of the harems, and historians refer to this period as 'the Rule of the Women', with a succession of ambitious wives and mothers distracting the sultans from affairs of state with sensual pleasures. Civil unrest further weakened the empire and it became known as 'The Sick Old Man of Europe', losing many of its territories, until its disastrous alliance with Germany in World War I finished it off completely.

Tomb of Mehmet the Conqueror, Fatih Camii, Istanbul

Politics

Background

Generally ranked as a 'developing country' by economists and sociologists, Turkey's recent political history, unlike such nations as Nigeria, India or Brazil, does not fit the standard role model for such a description.

Not shaped by any imperialist power of the 19th or 20th centuries, the modern Turkish state has evolved from its own Ottoman legacy. Its political problems during this century therefore stem largely from the decline and disintegration of its empire over the previous two centuries, with the gradual breakdown of the complex Ottoman administrative and military systems.

Government

A National Assembly of 450 members is elected by universal adult suffrage for a five-year term. The President is then elected in turn by the Assembly for a seven-year term. The current President is Süleyman Demirel, and the current Prime Minister is Tansu Çiller. Demirel, deposed by military coups in 1971 and 1980, is a veteran of Turkish politics, while Çiller, the first woman Prime Minister, only entered the political arena in 1991. A 47-year-old American-educated economist with good English, she represents a complete break from Turkey's old guard politicians. The hope is that Mrs Çiller will speed up Turkey's long overdue economic reforms, and her election is seen as a decisive step by Turkey away from the Islamic politics of the Middle East.

Political parties

The major parties are the centre-right True Path Party (DYP), now led by Tansu Çiller; the Motherland Party (ANAP), led by Mesut Yılmaz, and supporting monetarist economic policies, traditional nationalism and closer ties with the Islamic world; the Social Democratic People's Party (SHP), a left-wing party supporting liberal social reforms, with many Kurdish members; and the Welfare Party, an Islamic Conservative party.

Political issues

The hardest tasks facing the present government are how to tackle inflation, which currently runs at 70 per cent plus, and how to resolve Kurdish insurgency in the southeast. On the first task, Mrs Çiller's main policy objective is to embark on radical privatisation of the loss-making state industries. On the second task, she is known to be a hard-liner against Kurdish aspirations for antonomy, a stance she may have to modify if Kurdish groups carry out their promises to attack economic targets within the country.

Unstable coalitions in the 1970s are largely blamed for pushing Turkey into economic crisis, urban violence and then martial law in the 1980 coup. Turkey has frequently been criticised for its poor human rights record, and a new cabinet post of Minister for Human Rights has

> **WOMEN'S VOTE**
> Turkish women over 18 were given full suffrage in 1923 under Atatürk's reforms, something which their British counterparts did not achieve until 1928.

Tansu Çiller, Turkey's first woman prime minister, was elected in 1993 following the sudden death of President Turgut Özal and his succession by the then Prime Minister Süleyman Demirel

been created in a move to gain greater acceptance by a sceptical western Europe.

Turkey's foreign policy has taken a new direction in these post-Communist days, with Turkish influence extending as far as the 100 million Turkic speakers in the new Muslim republics of Central Asia and the Muslim parts of the Balkans, who all see Turkey as a role model of how to combine Muslim beliefs with modern social and economic policies. Turkey's strategic position as Europe's link with the Asian world has never been more crucial to a peaceful 21st century than it is now.

Culture

Origins

Modern Turks are descendants of the Turkish tribes from Central Asia who entered Anatolia during the 11th to 13th centuries and interbred with the ancient native stock of the region. Although the Turks were converted to Islam during these centuries, their distinctive language and popular culture makes them identifiably separate from the rest of the Muslim world. Immigrants from Balkan countries also play a substantial role in the nation's life. There is a sizeable Kurdish population, around 7 per cent, primarily located in the southeast.

Character

In defiance of all its Oriental associations, Turkey is an efficient place, where trains and buses run on time, and

where people say what they mean. There is no deviousness in the Turkish character and you will be told a straightforward no if something you have asked for is not possible, rather than fobbed off with promises and assurances.

In public, Turks appear dour – there is not much laughter in the streets – but their sense of humour is real enough. It just takes some knowing. Their reserved manner led them to be dubbed 'the Englishmen of the East' by early travellers. Though generally long-suffering and patient, the Turks have a capacity for violent reaction when pushed too far. Turkish soldiers are regarded as among the toughest in the world, and a two-year military service is mandatory.

The Turks are extremely proud of their country and its past, and Atatürk's slogan *'Ne mutlu Türküm diyene'* ('How happy is he who can say he is a Turk') is blazoned on hillsides and strung on banners on public holidays. With this nationalistic pride goes a belief in a Turcocentric universe and an excessive sensitivity to criticism, as evidenced by the Turkish attitude to the Armenian and Kurdish questions.

Honour and virility are the two most highly prized qualities, and Turkey is still an essentially male society. In a Turkish prison, the thief is the lowest form of life, while the murderer is the élite. Motives for murder are generally to do with honour, and therefore respected. For example, the un-premeditated murder of a faithless wife and her lover by a

The Military Museum Band dressed in bright traditional uniforms

Blue charms to protect against the 'Evil Eye', the spells cast over one by an ill-wisher

Cotton-picking near Pamukkale in the Aegean region of Turkey

wronged husband are seen as personal honour avenged.

The influence of Islam remains strong, and beads to ward off the evil eye can still be seen in most cars and taxis. Alcohol is consumed in moderation and public drunkeness is unheard-of. Young Turks are very keen to be educated, and the Turkish workforce is highly educated, with a higher number of graduates per capita than some northern European countries. The quality of education remains unevenly spread, with the already favoured western areas receiving the lion's share of teachers and resources at the expense of the provincial east.

Country versus city

The gulf between the rich and poor in Turkey is noticeable, particularly as you travel further east. About half the country's workforce is engaged in agriculture and lives in rural areas, while the other half is employed in heavy industry and manufacturing in the city factories. In recent years the trend has been towards urban migration, with the rural poor searching for better lifestyles in the city. This has led to the growth of vast shanty suburbs round the main cities of Istanbul, Ankara, Izmir and Adana. With this agricultural-industrial balance, Turkey is unusually self-sufficient, in food and in manufacturing, and its pride in this is almost tangible. Oil is its only serious deficiency, as it produces less than 20 per cent of its needs. The country has vast potential for economic development, but so far mismanagement and fear of disturbing the vested interests of a powerful élite has held it back from realising this potential.

Geography

Landscape and topography

Modern Turkey is a country with an area of 779,452 sq km, six times that of Greece, yet with half the number of people per square kilometre. The population is estimated at around 57 million, projected to rise to 70 million by the year 2000. The Anatolian peninsula has strongly defined geographical limits: the Kara Deniz (Black Sea) to the north; the Aegean in the west and the Mediterranean in the south; and the high mountain ranges that culminate in Büyükağrı Dağı (Mount Ararat) at 5,165m, to the east. The 5 per cent that lies west of the Çanakkale Boğazı (Dardanelles) is flatter, geographically a part of Europe, and contains the cities of Istanbul and Edirne. Its limit is defined by an artificial border whose exact position has varied considerably according to the politics of the day.

The main land mass consists of the bleak Steppelands of the central Anatolian Plateau, set at 1,000m, ringed by the verdant Pontic mountains to the north and the Toros (Taurus) to the south. These ranges run east to west and join up with the vast inhospitable mountainous region in the east that borders Iran and Iraq.

Volcanoes and earthquakes

There are several large volcanoes in Turkey besides Mount Ararat, the highest, but none are thought to be still active. Fault lines do still have movement and earthquakes in the north and west of Turkey have been commom throughout history and continue to strike every ten years or so. Both the Boğazıçı (Bosphorus) and the Dardanelles owe their existence to the shifting fault lines, and the whole of the Black Sea was created as a result of subsidence along a series of fissures.

Lakes and rivers

This rugged topography has created many lakes, far more than anywhere else in the region. Van Gölü (Lake Van) is the largest, seven times bigger than Lake Geneva. Turkey also boasts the sources of the Dicle (Tigris), 2,800km long, and the Fırat (Euphrates), 1,900km long.

Climate

The fertile coastal lowlands contrast dramatically with the mountainous interior, and this can lead to enormous seasonal variations in temperature. In the east, winter temperatures can go as low as -40°C with snow lying for 120 days of the year, while the Aegean coastal regions have mild rainy winters and summer temperatures around 35°C. Rainfall is highest along the Black Sea Coast.

Coastal landscape at Anamur

First Steps

'I have lived 80 years in
Istanbul and I do not
know the city. I have
spent 73 of them in
the Bazaar and I do not
know it either.'

CARPET SELLER
in the Covered Bazaar (1980)

Sirkeçi, Istanbul's railway station on the European side

BODY LANGUAGE

Turks say 'no' (*hayır* or *yok*) by lifting the head backwards, a gesture easily mistaken for yes.

Turks say 'yes' (*evet*) by nodding the head down.

Shake your head from side to side to signify you do not understand.

Finger pointing, public nose-blowing, public kissing or hugging of the opposite sex are considered offensive. An overfirm handshake is thought impolite.

Women should avoid too much eye contact with male strangers as this can be misread as encouragement instead of normal social behaviour. Western pornography and films have done much to foster the view that western women are 'available'. Women walking alone or even in pairs late at night are regarded as inviting male attention.

CRIME AND SECURITY

Crime rates are very low, far lower than in western countries, though pickpocketing and petty theft have increased since the advent of tourism. Beware especially in crowded centres like the Kapalıçarşı (Covered Bazaar) of Istanbul. Horror stories of westerners being clapped in prison only apply to those who are found carrying drugs or have seriously infringed the law.in some way

Never risk photography when it is expressly forbidden by a notice. Travel all over Turkey is unrestricted and safe. The only proviso is in the southeast regions like Hakkari, where Kurdish rebels are still active so it is advisable to stick to the main roads. As far as is known, no tourist has ever been injured in Kurdish incidents.

DRIVING

Traffic drives on the right so all cars are left-hand drive. Driving habits and styles are less disciplined than western Europe or North America, but relatively orderly compared to most Middle Eastern countries. Pedestrian crossings are a rarity and the driver always has right of way over the pedestrian. Signposting is good and road conditions are generally fine, though potholes are a regular feature east of Ankara.

GETTING AROUND

In Istanbul, car hire would be a mistake as there are so many taxis on the streets that are both cheaper and easier, saving you the headache of navigation. Taxis are all metered and tipping is not usual. Outside Istanbul it is definitely best to hire a car, as so many interesting places in Turkey lie off the main roads. If funds cannot run to this, bus is the next best, and all major cities and towns in Turkey are linked by excellent cheap and efficient bus services, clean and air-conditioned. Hitch-hiking is possible but not common, and is not advisable for women alone. (See also Practical Guide, entries for Driving and Public Transport).

LANGUAGE

English and German are widely spoken and understood, especially in the big cities and in the Aegean and Mediterranean tourist centres. Turks learn English as their first foreign language at school. Lack of Turkish is therefore not a problem unless you are travelling in remoter or eastern parts (see **Practical Guide**, Language entry for useful words and phrases). Since Atatürk in the 1920s, Turkish has used the Latin alphabet (like English) with

Tram at Taksim Square, Istanbul

just a few extra symbols like umlauts (¨) to cope with different vowel sounds. Turkish is a Ural-Altaic language unrelated to European languages or to Arabic. It has an extremely complex grammar.

Taking a rest outside the Fatih Camii, Istanbul

ATATÜRK: ISLA

Turkey is unique in the Muslim world as a model of a multi-party democracy. Religion is divorced from government and affairs of state, and this can be credited to one man, Kemal Atatürk, 'Father of the Turks' (1881–1938). A military hero, he organised the growing Turkish nationalist movement into a concerted rejection of the Allies' proposed carve-up of the Ottoman Empire. His efforts were crowned by the 1923 Treaty of Versailles which recognised Turkish sovereignty over what are approximately its present-day borders.

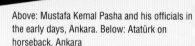

Above: Mustafa Kemal Pasha and his officials in the early days, Ankara. Below: Atatürk on horseback, Ankara

During the remaining 15 years of his life Atatürk carried out a series of far-reaching reforms designed to westernise Turkey and integrate it into the modern world. He terminated the caliphate, exiled the sultan, abolished the Ministry of Religious Affairs, disbanded religious orders, sequestrated religious property and forbade religious instruction. In 1928 Islam was disestablished and the constitution proclaimed Turkey a secular state.

Atatürk did not oppose religion itself, merely its interference in government. He held that everyone could be a devout Muslim in his private life, but that politics was a separate

A SECULAR STATE

matter for public debate. In modern Turkey politicians find this a difficult line to follow, as they recognise the power of Islam, particularly in the countryside. At election time, therefore, there is invariably some pandering to religious traditionalism to secure the rural vote.

Among the people themselves the country-city divide endures, and city-dwelling Turks tend to be low-key about their adherence to Islam. In the villages, religion still plays an important role, but there is nothing like the wave of fundamentalism that some alarmist media reports like to imagine.

The memory of Atatürk is everywhere – his portrait hangs in every public place, his statue stands in every town square and his face is on all stamps and banknotes.

Top: Atatürk Monument, Taksim Square, Istanbul.

Above: the blue-eyed 'Father of the Turks' and the Turkish flag

ISLAM

The word Islam itself means 'submission' in Arabic, and Muslims are those who submit themselves to Allah, the One True God, who is the same God as in Christianity and Judaism. The sacred book of Islam is the Koran which was revealed by divine inspiration through the mouthpiece of the Prophet Muhammad. Muhammad was not divine, he was the last of the prophets. Jesus Christ is recognised as a prophet but not as divine. This is a major point on which Islam diverges from Christianity, Muslims viewing the Christian Holy Trinity as heretical and as infringing the oneness of God. The Five Pillars or essential duties of Islam are first, to declare the creed 'There is no god but God and Muhammad is the messenger of God', second is to pray five times a day, third is to pay the *zakat*, or alms tax, fourth is to fast in Ramadan, and fifth is to visit Mecca at least once in a lifetime.

Facing east towards Mecca, midday prayers near the Covered Bazaar, Istanbul

Calls to prayer

You will hear these broadcast by loudspeaker from the minarets, and they can sound enchanting in large cities where all the mosques start within moments of each other. The call to prayer is sung in a ritualised chant, a much-prized art which the *muezzin* (the caller) takes years to perfect. Muslims pray five times a day: at dawn, at midday, mid-afternoon, sunset and before bed. The Friday noon prayer is the essential congregational prayer, when mosques are full. During prayers the believers must face Mecca, a direction indicated by the prayer niche (*mihrab*) in each mosque.

Mosque etiquette

Before stepping on a mosque's carpets, always remove your shoes and leave them in the racks provided outside. Women should wear a scarf to cover their hair. Avoid visiting mosques on Fridays or at prayer times. Most large city mosques close to non-Muslims from 12noon till 1pm for noonday prayers.

Ramadan

This is the Muslim month of fasting when, in certain places such as holy cities like Konya, visitors may

Mosque geography	
mihrab	prayer niche in wall of mosque that faces Mecca.
minbar	pulpit from which sermons are preached.
medrese	theological school attached to a mosque.
imaret	soup kitchen attached to mosque for feeding poor.
türbe	mausoleum

Religious devotion in the Eyüp Camii, Istanbul's holiest mosque

experience difficulty getting food and drink during daylight hours. Ramadan is a moveable feast following the lunar calendar, so the date changes every year. Muslims fast from dawn to dusk, then break the fast each evening with large amounts of feasting and celebrating which continue late into the night. Children, pregnant women, the old and the sick, and people on long journeys are exempted from the fast. The test of will-power is especially tough on the women, who have to continue to prepare meals for the children and elderly during the day, then have to prepare the main evening feast for the men. The exact age at which children have to start fasting remains a matter of individual choice, but is generally after eight.

In Istanbul and the Aegean and Mediterranean regions, restaurants remain open as usual during Ramadan and visitors would barely notice anything different. In the east it is more strictly observed and many restaurants will shut during the day, while only a few of the bigger hotels will serve alcohol.

The Sunni/Shia divide

Ninety-nine per cent of Turks are Sunni Muslims, that is the conservative orthodox majority, following the 'Sunna' or trodden path. The Sunni/Shia divide is the major sectoral split in Islam, as the Protestant/Catholic split is in Christianity. The divide dates back to the years immediately after Muhammad's death in 632 when the Shia supported Muhammad's son-in-law Ali and his descendants as the true successors, while the Sunnis believed the succession should be decided by the Islamic clergy. The Shia are the more outspoken element today, but account for only 10 per cent of Muslims worldwide. Most are to be found in Iran, Iraq, Pakistan and India.

Sailing yachts moored near Marmaris

ITINERARIES

Turkey lends itself very well to touring holidays and visitors can cover an amazing range of places. When planning more detailed visits, remember that museums are invariably shut on Mondays throughout the country. The following are feasible two-week itineraries assuming you have your own transport and that you are returning to the same airport. Some companies allow you to hire a car at one airport and return it at another, which obviously allows a lot more flexibility. If you are using public transport the same itinerary would probably take two or three days longer.

Tour 1
Istanbul (3 days), Bursa, Troy (Truva), Pergamum, Kuşadası, Ephesus (Efes), Priene, Miletos (Milet), Didyma, Bodrum (2 days), Pamukkale (2 days), Sardis (Sardes), Izmir, Balıkesir, Iznik, Istanbul.

Tour 2
Izmir, Kuşadası, Ephesus, Priene, Miletos, Didyma, Bodrum (2 days), Marmaris (2 days), Fethiye, Kalkan, Kaş, Antalya, Pamukkale (2 days), Izmir.

Tour 3
Antalya, Perge, Aspendos, Side (2 days), Alanya, Anamur, Silifke, Ürgüp (3 days), Konya (2 days), Eğirdir, Antalya.

Tour 4
Ankara (2 days), Boğazkale, Amasya, Sivas, Divriği, Elazığ, Diyarbakır, Şanlı Urfa, Nemrut Dağı, Adana, Ürgüp (2 days), Ankara.

Tour 5
Trabzon (2 days), Artvin, Kars, Ani, Doğubayazıt, Van (2 days), Diyarbakır, Mardin, Nemrut Dağı, Malatya, Erzincan, Erzurum, Sumela, Trabzon.

The Turkish flag

WHAT TO SEE

'You may have seen
amphitheatres in Italy,
France, Dalmatia and
Africa; temples in Egypt
and Greece; palaces in
Crete; you may be sated
with antiquity, or scornful
of it. But you have not
seen the theatre of
Aspendos'.

DAVID HOGARTH,
archaeologist (1909)

Istanbul

*H*ere is one of the world's most magical and evocative cities, viewed by the west as the gateway to the east with all its tantalising promise. It is neither European, nor Asian, nor Middle Eastern, but has flavours of all three.

The only city to stand astride two continents, Istanbul's unique geographical location lies at the heart of the city's magic. Europe is separated from Asia by the hilly straits of the Boğazıçı (Bosphorus), and different parts of the European city are separated by the inlet of the Haliç (Golden Horn), one of the world's most sheltered harbours. This abundance of water everywhere, the fact that you are always crossing bridges and catching boats, is Istanbul's other special charm.

It has been the capital of three world empires, the Roman, the Byzantine and the Ottoman, and has borne three names, Byzantium, Constantinople and Istanbul. For nearly 1,000 years it was the most important city in the western and near-eastern worlds

Political power moved to Ankara in 1923, along with all the government ministries and embassies, leaving Istanbul for the first time in 16 centuries without the status of capital of an empire. But for all that, Istanbul remains Turkey's cultural and commercial capital, generating some 40 per cent of Gross National Product.

The city has doubled its population every 15 years since 1950 because of rural migration to the city. The next census, due in 2000, will definitely yield a figure in excess of 10 million. Its infrastructure, not surprisingly, has been unable to keep pace, and there is terrific pressure on roads and services. There are sprawling dormitory suburbs,

unplanned and unsightly, though the average visitor will be blissfully unaware of them.

ISTANBUL LANDMARKS AND ORIENTATION

Ayasofya and Sultanahmet Camii (Blue Mosque)

Ayasofya has four minarets and the Blue Mosque has six, the obvious difference when viewed from a distance.

The whole precinct from Ayasofya to the Topkapı Sarayı (Topkapı Palace) and from Ayasofya to the Blue Mosque is pedestrianised, and makes pleasant strolling, especially since the addition of carefully landscaped gardens.

Besides these three great monuments, this hub of the city also has many smaller places of interest. In front of the Blue Mosque is the Hippodrome, the ancient sports and civic centre of Byzantium. Chariot races and circuses were held here, and the total capacity has been estimated at 100,000 spectators. The obelisk here is only the upper third of the original, which broke during shipment from Egypt. (See Aya Sofya, pages 30–1, Sultanahmet Camii, page 37).

Beyoğlu

This district is the quaint 19th-century European city, much of which has been turned into a pedestrian precinct. This is where most embassies and consulates are based.

Bosphorus and its two bridges

This is the strait that separates Europe
from Asia (see The Bosphorus By Boat,
pages 54–5). The first bridge, built in
1973, is called Boğazıçı Köprüsü, and
the second, completed in 1988 to relieve
traffic congestion on the first, is called
Fatih Sultan Mehmet Köprüsü, and
spans the straits further north between
the famous fortresses of Rumeli Hisar
and Anadolu Hisar, the same place
where the Persian Emperor Darius built
his bridge of boats in 512BC.

Bozdoğan Kemeri (Aqueduct of Valens)

This imposing landmark spans Atatürk
Bulvarı (Atatürk Boulevard) and still
stands to its full height in double arches.
It was built by the Emperor Valens in
AD375.

Column of Constantine

This porphyry column stands in solitary
splendour between the Grand Bazaar
and the Çemberlitaş Baths and is the
oldest remnant of Roman Byzantium. It
was erected by Constantine in AD330 as
a dedication to the city.

Divan Yolu

This is the main road along the top of
the hills of Stamboul, old Istanbul,
linking the Covered Bazaar area of
Beyazıt to the Sultanahmet district. A
modern tram now runs along it, and
much of it is pedestrianised.

Eminönü Meydanı (Eminönü Square)

Considered the heart of the city by its
inhabitants, this is the bustling square
below the Topkapı, where the Galata
Köprüsü (bridge) spans the Golden
Horn. The boat stations are all here, as
is the European railway station, Sirkeci.

Haliç (Golden Horn)

This inlet of the Bosphorus is crossed by
three bridges, the Galata, beside
Eminönü Square, the Atatürk that runs
up and under the Aqueduct of Valens,
and the Fatih Köprüsü (Haliç motorway
bridge), the furthest north, which runs
from the airport to the first Bosphorus
Bridge.

Kapalıçarşışı (Covered Bazaar)

This is the opposite of a landmark, as it
is invisible except from the air! You have
to search for it and cannot see it until
you are inside. (See A Walk Around the
Covered Bazaar, pages 50–1).

Stamboul

This is the western way of referring to
the old city that was the original
Constantinople, that is, the area where
Aya Sofya, the Blue Mosque, the
Topkapı and the Süleymaniye still stand
today.

Üsküdar

This important suburb of Istanbul lies
on the Asian side of the Bosphorus,
directly opposite the mouth of the
Golden Horn. Ferries run from the
Galata Bridge every 15 minutes to reach
Üsküdar. (See Atik Valide Camii and
Şemsi Pasa Camii, pages 36–7, and
Karaca Ahmet cemetery, pages 42–3.)

GETTING AROUND ISTANBUL

The best way to get around in
Istanbul is to walk whenever possible
and to catch taxis or ferries when not.
It is not worth hiring a car, as parking
is always tricky, and you will waste a
lot of time getting lost.

ISTANBUL

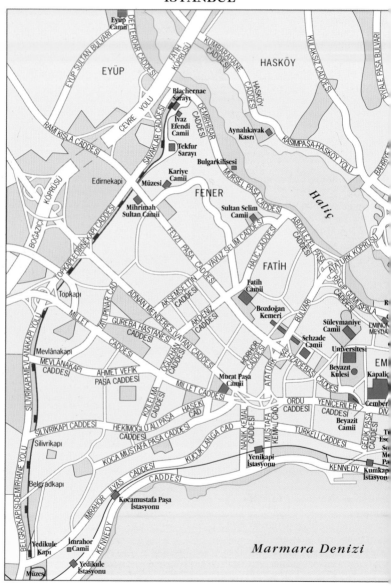

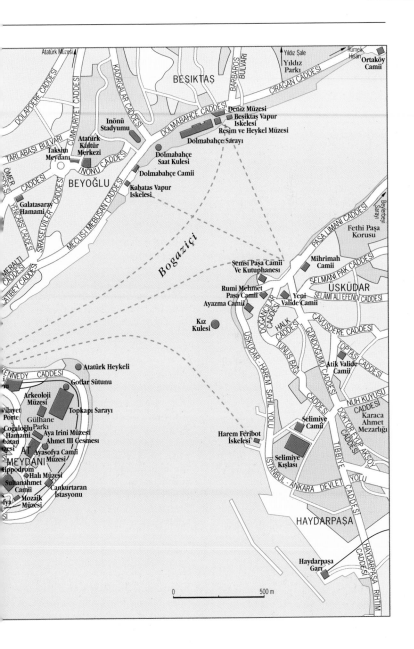

Atatürk Müzesi

Yıldız Şale

Yıldız Parkı

Rumeli Hisarı

Ortaköy Camii

BEŞİKTAŞ

KADIRGALAR CADDESİ

DOLAPDERE CADDESİ

CUMHURİYET CADDESİ

BARBAROS BULVARI

CIRAGAN CADDESİ

DOLMABAHÇE CADDESİ

Deniz Müzesi

İnönü Stadyumu

Beşiktaş Vapur İskelesi

Atatürk Kültür Merkezi

Resim ve Heykel Müzesi

TARLABAŞI BULVARI

Dolmabahçe Sarayı

Taksim Meydanı

İNÖNÜ CADDESİ

Dolmabahçe Saat Kulesi

ÖMER CADDESİ

BEYOĞLU

Dolmabahçe Camii

Galatasaray Hamamı

TÜNCARİ CADDESİ

SIRASELVİLER CADDESİ

MECLİSİ MEBUSAN CADDESİ

Kabataş Vapur İskelesi

Beylerbeyi Sarayı

MERALTİ CADDESİ

KATİBEY CADDESİ

Boğaziçi

PAŞA LİMANI CADDESİ

Fethi Paşa Korusu

Şemsi Paşa Camii Ve Kutuphanesı

Mihrimah Camii

SELMANİ PAK CADDESİ

ÜSKÜDAR

Rumi Mehmet Paşa Camii

Yeni Valide Camii

SELAMİ ALİ EFENDİ CADDESİ

Ayazma Camii

DOĞANCILAR CADDESİ

HALK CADDESİ

ÇAVUŞDERE CADDESİ

Kız Kulesi

ÜSKÜDAR-HAREM SAHİL YOLU

YUNUS BAĞ

GÜNDOĞUMU CADDESİ

TOPTAŞI CADDESİ

KENNEDY CADDESİ

Atatürk Heykeli

Gotlar Sütunu

Atik Valide Camii

Arkeoloji Müzesi

Topkapı Sarayı

NUH KUYUSU CADDESİ

Vilayet Porte

Gülhane Parkı

Selimiye Camii

DOKTOR EYÜP AKSOY CADDESİ

Karaca Ahmet Mezarlığı

Çağaloğlu Hamamı

Aya İrini Müzesi

Ahmet III Çeşmesi

batanı

Ayasofya Camii

Müzesi

Harem Feribot İskelesi

AT MEYDANI

Hipodrom

Halı Müzesi

Selimiye Kışlası

İSTANBUL-ANKARA DEVLET YOLU

TIBBIYE CADDESİ

Sultanahmet Camii

Mozaik Müzesi

Çankurtaran İstasyonu

fya

HAYDARPAŞA

Haydarpaşa Garı

HAYDARPAŞA CADDESİ

HAYDARPAŞA RIHTIM

0   500 m

Ayasofya Camii

(Cathedral of St Sophia)

*T*here can be few places with such an overwhelming sense of history. On entering, the interior is magnificent and awesome. Here is the centre of what was Byzantine Constantinople, an extraordinary building whose history is the very mirror of Byzantium itself.

Dedicated to Saint Sophia, the Divine Wisdom, by the Emperor Justinian in AD537, the current building is the last of three churches on this site. The first two were both destroyed by fire. Architecturally it is extremely complex and the vast shallow dome caused enormous structural stresses which have made it vulnerable to earthquake damage throughout its history. To compensate, the massive flying buttresses were added.

When the Crusaders sacked Constantinople in 1204 they stripped the interior of all removables and it then served as the Roman Catholic cathedral of the city throughout the Crusader occupation. The 15th century saw Constantinople in decay, and the

cathedral too fell to ruin. The last Christian service was held here in 1453, the day before the Turks took the city.

When the conquering Sultan Mehmet II entered the city on that day, he rode straight to St Sophia and ordered it to be converted immediately into a mosque. The following Friday the first Muslim prayers were held in it. Minarets, a *mihrab* and a *minbar* were added soon after, and the conversion was complete. Of the four minarets, the brick one was built first. The other three stone ones at the corners were added by Sinan in the 16th century.

The building was well maintained throughout the Ottoman period and successive sultans ordered restorations. The mosaics were covered with whitewash which helped a great deal to preserve them in the state we see today.

The mosque has been a museum since 1934. As you enter, look out for the immense doors sheathed in bronze which date back to Justinian's time. The stonework in the nave interior is breathtaking, especially the colossal columns of purple porphyry and dark green verd antique marble. This verd antique is known to have been specially quarried for the cathedral from Thessaly. The porphyry, which must have come from Egypt where the only quarries for this volcanic marble are to be found, is thought to have been taken

---

SINAN

Sinan is unquestionably the greatest Muslim architect. A near contemporary of Michaelangelo, he is credited with 81 large mosques, 50 smaller mosques, 19 mausoleums, 32 palaces, 22 public baths, two bridges and six aqueducts: 84 of his buildings are still standing in Istanbul alone. He was born of Greek Christian parents in 1491 and later assigned to the Janissaries as a military engineer. He was nearly 50 when he completed his first mosque, and he died aged 97.

from another more ancient building. The columns are topped with magnificent capitals carved in acanthus leaves. Throughout the church a colossal variety of rare and beautiful marble has been used.

A few mosaics have survived at the lower levels, notably the Virgin Mary with the Christ Child on her knees, but the most magnificent are in the galleries, which are reached by a cobbled ramp that zigzags upwards. These galleries were used for the imperial family and other dignitaries. The most famous gallery mosaic, not to be missed, is the Deesis with Christ in the centre, the Virgin Mary on one side, and an agonised John the Baptist on the other.

Scattered in the precincts outside are several domed imperial Ottoman tombs. *Aya Sofya Camii, Sultanahmet. Open: Tuesday to Sunday, 9am–5.30pm. Closed: Monday. Admission charge. Entry is from the Aya Sofya Meydani side, that is, the side facing the Blue Mosque.*

Above and below: the vast interior of Ayasofya Camii, the dome of which was such an architectural marvel of its time that people were afraid to enter for fear of its collapse

ISTANBUL CHURCHES

AYA IRINI (ST IRENE)
This vast and peaceful basilica is second
in size only to Aya Sofya, yet is easily
missed on the walk up to the Topkapı,
as it lies in a corner of the outermost
fourth court of the palace. As a result,
though thousands walk by it every day, it
remains a tranquil haven. A cobbled
ramp leads down into the vast interior.
Its name, suitably, means Divine Peace.
The current building dates from the 6th
century. The Turks used it as an arsenal
for the Janissaries, the military élite
guard of the sultan who were barracked
in this court, and before the
Archaeological Museum was opened, it
was used to store antiquities. These days
it is used for exhibitions and concerts,
especially during the Istanbul Festival,
and the acoustics are said to be superb.
*Aya Irini Müzesi, close to the Topkapı
Palace entrance. Open: Tuesday to
Sunday, 9am–5pm. Closed: Monday.
Admission free.*

AYASOFYA (ST SOPHIA), see pages
30–1.

BULGAR KILISESI (ST STEPHEN OF THE BULGARS)
This remarkable church is made entirely
of cast iron, inside and out. It was
prefabricated in Vienna in 1871 then
shipped down the Danube and across
the Black Sea to be assembled here. It is
excellently maintained by the tiny
Bulgarian community which still
worships here regularly. Its location on
the western side of the Golden Horn
enhances its attractive appearance. A
guardian lives in a hut within its
railinged garden and will open the
church for a small consideration.

*Mürsel Paşa Caddesi, Fener. Open: always
when the guardian is in attendance.
Admission free, but leave a small tip.*

IMRAHOR CAMII (ST JOHN THE BAPTIST OF STUDIUS)
This vast ruined hulk is the oldest
surviving Christian monument in the
city, completed in AD463. Set in a
walled courtyard, it is still very
impressive, and the guardian family that
lives in the adjacent hut holds the key to
admit visitors. The church was once the
centre of a monastic community housing
1,000 monks.
*Imam Asir Sokak, near Yedikule. Open:
for a small tip to the guardian family.*

KARIYE CAMII (ST SAVIOUR IN CHORA)
After Ayasofya this is the most
important Byzantine church in the city,
now turned into a small museum to
display its own mosaic murals and
frescos, which are considered the finest
examples of Byzantine art in the world.

The church is set in a charming
courtyard at the opposite end of which is
an Ottoman house converted to a café.
It is a quiet spot away from the traffic,
with just a handful of stalls selling
upmarket souvenirs.

The name 'in Chora' means in the
country, for the church was originally
outside the city walls. The small scale of
the church, after the vast interiors of
Ayasofya and the imperial mosques,
makes the mosaics here seem very
accessible, almost intimate. The mosaics
date from the early 14th century. The
fact that they remain in such good
condition is thanks to the whitewash
spread on them during the centuries of
Ottoman rule when the church was a
mosque. The restoration work took 11

Harrowing of Hell, with Christ pulling Adam and Eve from their tombs, Kariye Camii

ears and was completed by the Byzantine Institute of America in 1958.

The mosaics relate the life story of the Virgin Mary and the life of Christ from infant to adult in unusual detail. Mary is rebuked in one scene by Joseph when he returns from a journey to find her pregnant. In the next scene he is reassured by a dream that she is telling the truth about the conception of her baby. Other striking scenes depict Christ's temptation by the devil and Christ's miracles, notably walking on water, the feeding of the 5,000, and turning the water into wine. There is also a startling resurrection scene with Christ pulling Adam and Eve from their tombs.

Near the Edirnekapı (Edirne Gate). Open: Wednesday to Monday, 9am–4.30pm. Admission charge.

KÜÇÜK AYASOFYA (SAINTS SERGIUS AND BACCHUS)

Converted to a mosque in the early 16th century and still in use today, this former church is one of the most beautiful Byzantine churches surviving in the city. Set down near the seafront below the Blue Mosque, the old quarter in which the mosque stands has wooden houses with carved overhanging balconies. The church was built by Justinian in AD527 before Aya Sofya, which it is said to resemble.

Inside, climb the stairs to the gallery for the best view of the church decorations. Peering out through the windows at the overgrown graveyard, the setting has an almost rural feel. *Küçük Ayasofya Caddesi, Sultanahmet. Open: always, like all working mosques. Admission free.*

THE BYZANTINE EMPIRE

In a move that symbolised the decline of Rome and the separation of the eastern and western halves of the Roman Empire, the Emperor Constantine founded in AD330 a new capital at Constantinople. While the western half collapsed in AD476, the eastern empire (called Byzantine after Byzantium, the Greek name for the earlier town on the site) survived until 1453, when the Ottoman Turks finally extinguished it.

The Byzantine Empire was left with two major legacies: the preservation of Greek culture and the creation of Orthodox Christianity as a state religion, with Byzantine emperors playing the roles of Caesar and Pope combined. These emperors, notably Justinian, provided lavish patronage for artists and architects, resulting in the development of the classic Byzantine domed basilica, of which the 6th–century Ayasofya is the most outstanding example (see pages 30–1). All Byzantine churches in Constantinople were built of brick, with little exterior decoration. Inside, by contrast, they were ablaze with colour from mosaics, often depicting biblical story cycles. In Ayasofya, only fragments of these mosaics are visible, but those in the church of St Saviour in Chora (now the Kariye Museum, see

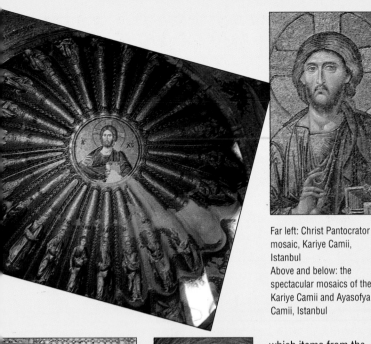

Far left: Christ Pantocrator
mosaic, Kariye Camii,
Istanbul
Above and below: the
spectacular mosaics of the
Kariye Camii and Ayasofya
Camii, Istanbul

which items from the Bible should be represented where in the church. All pictorial decorations were alas destroyed by the zealous Iconoclasts (image- or icon-breakers), whose hegemony lasted from AD711 until 843, which is why the extant mosaics in Istanbul today all date from the mid-9th century onwards.

pages 32–3) are recognised as the most stunning and complete example of Byzantine mosaic art. Veneration of icons (images of Christ, the Virgin and the saints) also began in the Byzantine era, and an elaborately stylised iconography developed to work out

The Byzantine style of art and architecture spread outwards to neighbouring regions, so we can still see domed churches of remarkable similarity across Italy, Greece and the Balkans, frequently decorated with mosaics and icons.

ISTANBUL MOSQUES

All these working mosques are open daily and can be visited except during the five periods of prayer. There are no entry fees but a small tip (*baksheesh*) is usually expected by the shoe attendant.

ATIK VALIDE CAMII

This rarely visited mosque dominates the skyline of Üsküdar, built in 1583 by Sinan. It has a lovely but neglected cloister courtyard.
Kartal Baba Caddesi, Üsküdar.

AYA SOFYA CAMII, see pages 30–31

BEYAZIT CAMII

Set on the hill between Istanbul University and the Covered Bazaar, the Beyazıt (built 1501) is the earliest imperial mosque extant in the city. The mosque has a scruffy but charming courtyard with fine porphyry, verd antique and granite columns and insets. The amount of colourful marble underfoot is a constant delight in Istanbul. Steps from the courtyard lead to the open yard under the famous plane tree where students gather for tea.

EYÜP SULTAN CAMII, see Sunset Walk from Pierre Loti's Café, pages 52–3.

FATIH CAMII

This mosque complex is the biggest and most elaborate in Istanbul and indeed in the entire Ottoman empire. Built by Mehmet the Conqueror in 1463, the Turkish name means conquest. The huge complex incorporates a *medrese*, hospices, a hospital, an *imaret*, a *caravanserai*, a *hamam* and a graveyard. Size is the distinguishing feature of the Fatih rather than architectural merit. Of the associated buildings, the hospice and hospital merit a visit for their beautiful courtyards.
Tophane Sokağı, Fatih. On one of the highest hills of Stamboul, north of the Süleymaniye Camii.

MIHRIMAH SULTAN CAMII (EDIRNE KAPI)

This exquisite mosque, raised up on a platform just inside the Edirne Gate, is one of Sinan's masterpieces, built for the Princess Mihrimah, Süleyman the Magnificent's favourite daughter. The guardian does not open it before 11am.

RÜSTEM PAŞA CAMII

Built in 1561, this is one of Sinan's finest small mosques. It is famous above all for the superb Iznik tiles that virtually cover the walls. Hidden in a side street up the hill from Eminönü Square, the mosque is entered by climbing internal steps beside some vaulted shops.

ŞEMSI PAŞA CAMII

This little gem built by Sinan of white stone in 1580 stands right on the edge of the water, at the confluence of the Bosphorus and the Sea of Marmara, on the Asian side.
Sahil Yolu, Üsküdar.

SOKULLU MEHMET PAŞA CAMII

This is considered the most beautiful of the smaller mosques of the city, built by Sinan in 1571. The charming courtyard is surrounded by the little domes of the *medrese* where children can still be seen learning the Koran by rote. Sokullu Mehmet was Grand Vizier (chief adviser) to Süleyman the Magnificent and his son Selim II. The small interior is exquisitely decorated, with Iznik tiles on the cone of the *minbar* and flanking it.

The gallery is for the women, who in fact only attend the mosque on special occasions. Above the door lintel is a small square fragment of the black Kaaba stone.

SÜLEYMANIYE CAMII

Prominent, with its four minarets, from most parts of Istanbul, this is regarded as the most beautiful imperial mosque of the city. It is a masterpiece of the great Ottoman architect, Sinan, and is a fitting testimony to its founder Süleyman the Magnificent, whose tomb and that of his wife Roxelana lie within the complex. The colossal dark grey stone mosque was finished in 1557 and took seven years in the building.

A first time visitor will be staggered by the sheer size of the mosque and its courtyard complex. All around the edge are arcaded old shops selling souvenirs, and some cafés.

The mausoleum is, as befits its occupant, the largest and grandest Sinan ever built. Sinan's own *türbe* lies in a modest corner just beyond the *caravanserai*. The other buildings round the precinct are the theological schools and primary schools, hospital, *hamam* and enormous public kitchens to feed the district's poor and the clergy staff, students, hospital patients as well as travellers in the *caravanserai*.
Şifahane Sokak, Süleymaniye. East up the hill from Eminönü Square.

SULTANAHMET CAMII (BLUE MOSQUE)

Completed in 1616, the Blue Mosque dominates the skyline of Istanbul with its six tall minarets, vying with the Süleymaniye for the title of supreme imperial mosque of Istanbul. During the centuries that the sultans resided at the

Topkapı Palace, an imperial procession would take place each Friday down to this mosque to attend the noonday prayers. The splendid ablution fountain in the centre of the monumental courtyard is still where the ritual washing before prayer takes place.

The interior is unusually light, with 260 windows. Some are stained glass, but the quality is very mixed. The predominant colour in the painted arabesques and the tiles is blue, giving the mosque its popular name. The Iznik tiles that cover the lower part of the walls are of the highest quality, in subtle blues and greens with elaborate floral designs of lilies, tulips and roses. The other striking internal features are the four marble columns supporting the dome, impressively huge with 5m diameters. *Mimar Mehmet Ağa Caddesi, Sultanahmet. Tourists are asked to use the entrance facing Ayasofya, and are confined to the back half of the mosque by railings.*

YENI CAMII (NEW MOSQUE)

Of no special architectural merit, this mosque, built in 1597, is well known because of its prominent location at Eminönü Square beside the Galata Bridge and the Egyptian Spice Market.

ROXELANA
Roxelana 'The Russian' was Süleyman the Magnificent's favourite wife. In her ambitions for her own son, Selim the Sot, she persuaded Süleyman to murder his elder son Mustafa, so that Selim could succeed to the throne. The drunken Selim's rule is generally reckoned as the beginning of the end for the Ottoman Empire.

ISTANBUL MUSEUMS

ARKEOLOJI MÜZESI (ARCHAEOLOGICAL MUSEUM) AND ESKI ŞARK ESERLERI MÜZESI (ANCIENT ORIENT MUSEUM)

The Archaeological Museum is a vast and fascinating place, boasting one of the richest collections in the world of Greco-Roman statues and antiquities, along with a remarkable collection of sarcophagi dating from the 4th century BC, discovered by a Turkish archaeologist at the royal necropolis of Sidon, Lebanon. One is known as the Alexander sarcophagus because of the battle scenes depicted on its sides. The halls on the ground floor contain Greek and Roman statues. The museum is now on several floors, but the ground floor remains the most impressive.

The Ancient Orient Museum is a fascinating and digestible display of ancient Egyptian, Babylonian and Hittite artefacts. Most memorable are the Hittite statues, from the colossal lions flanking the entrance to the sphinxes and larger-than-life storm gods inside. Among the most striking exhibits are the wall lions from Nebuchadnezzar's Babylon (5th century BC) made from colourful brick tiles, predominantly yellows and blues. *These two museums, together with the Çinili Köşk Museum, share a common admission charge and a lovely courtyard littered with vast sarcophagi and other architectural fragments. They also share a charming café set among the columns and statues. The joint courtyard of the museums lies within the Topkapı Palace walls, signposted down a lane from the Fourth Court. Open: Tuesday to Sunday, 9am–5.30pm. Closed: Monday.*

AYASOFYA MÜZESI, see pages 30–1.

ÇINILI KÖŞK (TILE KIOSK)

Today a museum of Turkish tiles and ceramics, this beautiful pavilion was built in 1472 as an outer pavilion of the Topkapı and is an exquisite oriental-looking edifice. Many of the rooms are themselves tiled, and the exhibits include tile panels from various mosques.
Topkapı Sarayı, Sultanahmet.

HALI MÜZESI (TURKISH CARPETS MUSEUM)

This houses a remarkable collection of carpets ranging from the 15th to the 19th centuries.
Kabasakal Caddesi, Sultanahmet (beside the Blue Mosque at the northeast corner). Open: Tuesday to Saturday, 9.30am–5.30pm. Closed: Sunday and Monday. Admission charge.

KARIYE MÜZESI (KARIYE MUSEUM), see pages 32–3.

MOZAIK MÜZESI (MOSAIC MUSEUM)

These are the *in situ* displays of mosaic pavements from the Great Palace of Byzantium, discovered in 1935. The mosaics are thought to date to AD500, showing animated scenes of Byzantine life.
Kabasakal Caddesi, Sultanahmet (behind the restored Ottoman street market by the Blue Mosque). Open: Wednesday to Monday, 9am–5pm. Closed: Tuesday. Admission charge.

SADBERK HANIM MÜZESI (SADBERK HANIM MUSEUM)

Located in a handsome *yalı* (summer

...ouse) on the upper Bosphorus shore between Büyükdere and Sarıyer, this museum houses a unique collection of Turkish works of art, founded by the wife of one of Turkey's leading business men.

Piyasa Caddesi, Büyükdere (a short walk north from Büyükdere landing stage). Open: Thursday to Tuesday, 10am–5pm. Admission charge.

TOPKAPI SARAYI MÜZESI (TOPKAPI PALACE MUSEUM),

see pages 44–5.

TÜRK-ISLAM ESERLERI MÜZESI (MUSEUM OF TURKISH AND ISLAMIC ART)

This splendid 19th-century palace is the grandest private residence ever built in the Ottoman Empire. Its attractive gallery overlooks the Hippodrome and the Blue Mosque and serves as a teahouse. It was the home of Ibrahim Pasha, Grand Vizier to Süleyman the Magnificent and married to Süleyman's sister. Süleyman's evil wife Roxelana convinced Süleyman that Ibrahim was becoming a threat to his own authority and so Süleyman dutifully arranged for his slaves to murder Ibrahim.

The interior courtyard of marble paving with a garden has been beautifully restored. The exhibits are extremely well displayed and include miniatures, manuscripts and calligraphy, ceramics and glass, woodwork and carpets. There is also an intriguing display of the tent-life of the nomadic Yürük, forbears of the Turks.

Binbirdirek (opposite the Blue Mosque beside the Hippodrome). Open: Tuesday to Sunday, 10am–5pm. Closed: Monday. Admission charge.

YEREBATAN SARAYI MÜZESI (UNDERGROUND MUSEUM)

This vast underground cistern should not be missed. Now fully restored, it was originally built in AD532 by Justinian to store water for the emperor's Great Palace. The entrance is only identifiable from the queue of people buying tickets, as nothing exists at ground level. There follows a slippery descent into the still water-filled cistern, with its total of 336 columns, by far the largest Roman cistern in the city. Opera music sets the atmosphere, and the only other sound is dripping water. The wooden walkways over the water are slippery and have meagre fencing, so keep a firm hold of excited children or elderly companions. Notice the upside down and sideways huge Medusa heads at the far end, clearly pilfered from an earlier temple, an unexpected sight in this unforgettable place.

The cistern was rediscovered in the 16th century when a local architect heard that the houses in the neighbourhood obtained their water by lowering buckets from their basements, sometimes catching fish in the process.

Yerebatan Caddesi, Sultanahmet (a short walk across the street from Aya Sofya Meydanı). Open: daily, 9am–5pm. Admission charge.

Archaeological Museum, Istanbul

ISTANBUL PALACES

AYNALIKAVAK KASRI (PALACE OF THE MIRRORING POPLARS)

This attractive late Ottoman palace has been restored with decor dating from the 19th century. It is renowned for its numerous windows, many of them stained glass. It is rarely visited because it lies off the tourist track on the eastern side of the Golden Horn.

Kasımpaşa-Hasköy Yolu, Hasköy (500m from the Hasköy landing stage on the Golden Horn). Open: Tuesday, Wednesday and Friday to Sunday, 9.30am–4pm. Admission charge.

BEYLERBEYI SARAYI (BEYLERBEYI PALACE)

This is the grandest palace ever built on the Asian side of Istanbul, intended as a summer palace for the later Ottoman sultans and a guesthouse for visiting royalty. Its interior is as lavish as that of the Dolmabahçe, and the architects of these two palaces were brothers. It is best reached by taking a ferry to Üsküdar, from where it is a five-minute taxi ride.

Abdullah Ağa Caddesi, Beylerbeyi (immediately north of the first Bosphorus Bridge, on the Asian side). Open: Tuesday, Wednesday and Friday to Sunday, 9am–12.30pm and 1.30pm–5pm. Admission charge.

BLACHERNAE SARAYI

Little survives of this Byzantine palace tucked in a poor quarter of the city just inside the walls. Recently landscaped with a children's playground, the best view of it is from the terrace of the adjacent Ivaz Efendi Mosque.

Toklu Dede Sokak, Ayvansaray (beside the Ivaz Efendi Mosque). Open: always. Admission free.

BUCOLEON SARAYI

All along the Sea of Marmara from Küçük Ayasofya Mosque to the Kalyon Hotel is a stretch of well-preserved Byzantine sea wall built by Constantine the Great. Set in these walls is a marble-sided arched gateway known as Çatladı Kapı, the Imperial Marine Gate, which was the entrance to the Bucoleon Palace Three marble-framed windows of the palace can be seen a little further west. This is all that now remains of Constantine's magnificent Great Palace of Byzantium, built when he first founde his new capital in AD330. It was sacked by the crusaders in 1204, and by the tim of the Turkish conquest in 1453 the palace was in ruins.

Bucoleon Caddesi, Kennedy Caddesi, Sultanahmet. Open: always. Admission free

ÇIRAĞAN SARAYI (ÇIRAĞAN KEMPINSKI HOTEL)

Gutted by fire in 1910, this palace stood as a ruined shell for decades, until it was recently renovated to become arguably the most luxurious hotel in Istanbul.

Çirağan Kempinski Oteli, Çirağan Caddesi, Beşiktaş (on the Bosphorus at the foot of the Yıldız Park). The bars and restaurants are open to non-residents.

DOLMABAHÇE SARAYI (DOLMABAHÇE PALACE)

The most fabulously lavish palace in Turkey with a breathtaking 600m frontage on to the Bosphorus, this white marble rococo-style palace was commissioned by Sultan Abdul Mejid in 1834 after he had become depressed by living in the Topkapı Palace and desired a change. The architect was a Turkish Armenian. The sultans of the later years of the Ottoman Empire all moved here, leaving the Topkapı abandoned

Bosphorus frontage of the Dolmabahçe Palace

up on the hill.

Once into the gardens, where there is a pleasant café and souvenir shop, all is peaceful away from the traffic noise. Head for the palace itself, where conducted tours head off round the interior every 15 minutes and last nearly an hour.

The official rooms are still sometimes used for special functions, and the elaborately ornate decoration is reminiscent of French palaces like Versailles. The bird pavilion still houses species from all over the world.

Dolmabahçe Caddesi, Beşiktaş (500m from the Kabataş landing stage on the European side of the Bosphorus). Open: Tuesday, Wednesday and Friday to Sunday, 9am–3pm. Admission charge (extra to use cameras or video cameras). The palace has a daily quota of 1,500 visitors and closes after this has been reached.

KÜÇÜKSU KASRI (LITTLE WATER PALACE)

Sometimes called Göksu Palace, this exquisite 19th-century rococo palace stands on the Asian Bosphorus shore between the streams known as the Sweet Waters of Asia. The Ottoman sultans used it for holidaying, and the meadows around are still popular for family picnics at weekends.

Küçüksu Caddesi, Göksu (just south of the new Bosphorus Bridge, on the Asian side, a short walk from Küçüksu landing stage). Open: Tuesday, Wednesday and Friday to Sunday, 9am–4pm. Admission charge.

TEKFUR SARAYI (PALACE OF THE PORPHYROGENITUS)

An unexpectedly magnificent façade of this Byzantine residence of the 13th century survives, tucked just inside the walls. Built of red brick and white marble, it still stands three storeys high.

Şişehane Caddesi, Avcı bey (west from Eğrikapı, inside the walls). Open: always. Admission free, but the resident guardian family expects a tip.

YILDIZ SARAYI (YILDIZ PALACE)

Set at the top of the magnificent Yıldız Park, this late 19th-century palace included a complex of pavilions and a mosque. Because of restoration work only one pavilion, the Şale, is open to the public at present.

Yıldız Caddesi, Yıldız (on the hill beyond Beyoğlu next to the Yıldız University). Open: Tuesday, Wednesday and Friday to Sunday, 9am–5pm. Admission charge.

ISTANBUL PARKS AND CITY WALLS

Istanbul is a city deceptively rich in parks and open spaces, and finding them is especially important if you have spent long spells in the bustling, overcrowded centres. All the parks mentioned are open to the public free of charge from 8am till dusk.

HALIÇ (GOLDEN HORN)

The whole western shoreline of the Golden Horn has been landscaped, making peaceful strolling whilst gazing at the impressive skyline of the old city (see pages 52–3). North of the new Galata Bridge you can see segments of the famous old Galata Bridge with its floating restaurants that had to be dismantled in May 1992, after a gas

explosion in one of the restaurants blew a hole in the middle of the bridge.

GÜLHANE PARKI (GÜLHANE PARK)

Once part of the Topkapı Palace, this is now a fine public park on the hillside below the palace. From the fountain outside the Topkapı walls, the main entrance to the park is reached by following the cobbled street that leads down Soğukçeşme Sokak past the old Ottoman houses which the Turkish Touring and Automobile Club has tastefully converted to hotels.

The southern end of the park is taken up by Istanbul Zoo. The zoo's aquarium is housed in a Roman cistern.

KARACA AHMET MEZARLIK (KARACA AHMET CEMETERY)

A lovely and unusual place for a stroll, this enormous graveyard in Üsküdar is the largest and oldest Muslim cemetery

The impressive walls of Rumeli Hisari the ruined 15th-century fortress on the Bosphorus

in Turkey. Take a ferry to Üsküdar, then a taxi up the hill to the Karaca Ahmet Camii, beside which is the main entrance to the cemetery.
Gündoğümü Caddesi, Üsküdar.

YILDIZ PARKI

A fabulously landscaped Ottoman park covering a hillside overlooking the Bosphorus, this is a tranquil place to stroll and sip tea in one of the beautifully restored kiosks or conservatories with dramatic Bosphorus views. It is easily the loveliest park in Istanbul.
Yıldız Caddesi, Yıldız.

THE CITY WALLS

The mighty land walls which protected the city of Byzantium from its enemies for over 1,000 years still stand for most of their 6.5km length. To walk along them these days is quite ambitious and should only be attempted when the weather has been dry for several consecutive days. In parts you can stroll along the ramparts, and where this is not possible, you have to judge whether it is more convenient to walk inside or outside the walls.

The land walls were originally built under Emperor Theodosius II (AD408–50), but earthquake damage caused them to be rebuilt later that century, when the outer wall and moat were added. There were a total of 96 defence towers. The moat, now destroyed in many places, used to be 20m wide and 10m deep and was flooded with water at times of danger.

The impregnability of these Byzantine land walls altered the course of history, when Attila the Hun, Scourge of God, thwarted by the power of the walls, directed his wrath instead on the western Roman Empire.

Today most people drive round the outside of the walls to get a feel of their scope, but the point at which you should certainly stop is Yedikule, the Castle of the Seven Towers, which stands near the Sea of Marmara, approached from Kennedy Caddesi. Part of the tower was used as a prison, part as storage for the state treasure. It was also the main place of execution, and instruments of torture used by the Ottomans are on display here. On the outer wall is the so-called Golden Gate, originally a Roman triumphal arch dated AD390. Its doors were originally covered in gold plate, but were later walled up for defence and never reopened.
Yedikule Müzesi, Kapı Yol, Yedikule.
Open: Tuesday to Sunday,
9.30am–4.30pm. Closed: Monday.
Admission charge.

Yıldız Park, one of the most beautiful green areas in Istanbul

Topkapı Sarayı

(Topkapı Palace)

*T*his palace is today an incomparable museum of Ottoman wealth and splendour, beautifully laid out in the palace rooms, a real feast for the eyes. The Topkapı has one of the most fabulous settings of any palace anywhere, on the promontory jutting out between the Bosphorous and the Golden Horn, the first hill of the Seven Hills of Istanbul which visitors have such difficulty identifying now.

The palace has four courtyards, and the entrance to the first one is marked by the fabulous free-standing rococo street fountain of Ahmet III with its own overhanging roof. Built in 1728, it is the most beautiful and elaborate Ottoman fountain in the city, as befits its location. The ticket office lies within the first court, the Court of the Janissaries, where the sultan's élite military corps of slave soldiers was stationed, forbidden

from entering the inner courts. In the extreme southeast corner stands the impressive basilica of St Irene. During confidential meetings with officials and dignitaries, the sultan would instruct the fountains to be turned on so that no one could overhear their discussions.

The entrance to the third court is flanked by two magnificent octagonal towers. The main walkway through is lined with cypress trees, two of which have curiously interbred with a fig and a plane tree to form hybrids. Byzantine cisterns run under this walkway, and traces of the red brickwork can still be seen under the paving. The harem lies over to the far western end of the courtyard and the separate ticket kiosk stands outside it.

Little is really known for sure about life in the harem. Much is gossip and hearsay. The women were guarded by black eunuchs, and even the chief physician was only allowed to inspect his patients' hands. Bananas and cucumbers, it is said, were only allowed in sliced. The lucky woman in favour on any particular night would be summoned to the imperial bedchamber, told to kiss the imperial coverlet at the foot end, then wriggle her way under it

Topkapı Palace, entrance to the third court

to encounter the sultan. No Turkish woman is thought ever to have had this honour, only thousands of Caucasians, Georgians and Armenians, and a handful of Western Europeans. Murat III (1574–95) had 1,200 harem women and fathered 103 children by them. Problems inevitably arose in such circumstances about how to decide the succession, and the usual Ottoman solution was wholesale slaughter of the other contenders by the eldest. When this custom was thought to be getting out of hand, a new method was introduced of locking up the younger brothers in the royal prison within the Topkapı, known as the Kafes. When the harem was disbanded by the Young Turks in 1909, circulars were sent out to outlying Caucasian villages of the empire, instructing parents to come and reclaim their daughters.

Next to the harem you will notice another separate kiosk for tours to the Halberdiers-with-Tresses' quarters. These men acted as porters and guards, and their weird uniform was a collar so high they could see neither to right nor left, wearing wool tresses on either side of their faces.

Within the palace, the kitchens occupy the biggest single building. There were 10 different ones, each catering for a different hierarchy. Today they house a priceless ceramics collection.

For most people the highlight of the museum is the Treasury, where the accumulated jewels and treasure of the Ottoman sultans are displayed. Here you can see some of the biggest emeralds and diamonds in the world, and the famous Topkapı dagger. It tends to be the most crowded part of the museum.

Beyond into the furthermost court are the ornate kiosks and terraces with

Topkapı Palace, the Treasury

fabulous views, where the restaurant and café make lingering even more of a pleasure.

Sultanahmet (tel: 512 04 80). Open: Wednesday to Monday, 9.30am–5pm. Admission charge. There is an additional charge for a tour of the Harem, queued for and bought separately inside the palace. Tours of the harem leave every 30 minutes, between 10am and 4pm. No tours between 12am and 1pm. The Topkapı lies within a pedestrian precinct area (except for taxis), just four minutes' walk north of Ayasofya.

Topkapı Palace, mosaics in the kiosks

THE TURKISH BATH

There are said to be about 100 old Ottoman baths, called *hamam* in Istanbul, of which about 80 are still in use. There is little doubt that they will survive into the 21st century, as the fuel shortage makes a weekly visit to the *hamam* an attractive proposition. The degree of all-over cleanliness it produces is way beyond what most of us ever achieve through our daily baths and showers. As a British reverend wrote in the 1930s during his stay here: 'They hold impurity of the body in greater detestation than impurity of the mind, ablution being so essential that without it prayer will be of no value in the eyes of God'. Ottoman marriage contracts stipulated that a husband had to give his wife bath-money. If he failed to do so it was grounds for divorce.

Mixed bathing is not permitted except in some of the larger hotels to accommodate foreigners' preferences, and the penalty for a man entering the woman's *hamam* used to be death. The women's baths are delightfully relaxing places, with fat homely masseuses in black briefs and colossal swinging bosoms, often smoking cigarettes in between customers. Nakedness is the norm among foreigners in a women's *hamam*. Since you are probably only going to do it once, have everything on offer – the rub with the rough glove to shed years of grime from your front and especially your back, the soaping, the face massage and even the foot

An Istanbul Turkish Bath by Thomas Allom, 1835

massage. Even with all the extras the whole experience is still remarkably good value. Each person has a locker for their valuables. The men's baths, by contrast, sound a lot less fun, with no singing, and towels wrapped firmly round waists.

The baths recommended for foreigners are the Çağaloğlu, the Çemberlıtas and the Çinili in Sultanahmet, and the Galatasaray in Beyoğlu. Some of the big five-star hotels also have small Turkish baths, but they lack the authentic atmosphere.

Top: Coy men of the Çembverlıtas Baths
Above: sitting-out room of the Galatasaray Baths
Left: Massage in action, Galatasaray Baths

ISTANBUL ENVIRONS

ADALAR (PRINCES' ISLANDS)

These nine islands, of which only four are inhabited, are an hour's ferry ride south from Istanbul, making popular weekend retreats. No cars are allowed, and the only means of transport for visitors and inhabitants alike is horse and carriage.

FERRIES
To save road distances there are several car ferries across the Sea of Marmara. The major ones are Eceabat-Çanakkale, Gelibolu-Lapseki and Pendik-Yalova. They all take about 30 minutes, are cheap and run throughout the day and evening.

Çanakkale Boğazıçı (The Dardanelles)

This is the ancient Hellespont, the straits that separate Europe from Asia. Legend has it that Leander reputedly swam across them each night to visit his lover Hero, until drowned in a storm. The endless coming and going of boats of all shapes and sizes can be watched from one of Çanakkale's seafront cafés.

BURSA

At four hours' drive each way, this is just feasible as a day trip from Istanbul, and many tour agencies indeed offer it. A spa town, most of the hotels have their own mineral water baths, but the town is mainly visited for its famous mosques.

Bedestan and Koza Han

Right in the centre of the city and recognisable by the two squat broad minarets of the adjacent Ulu Cami (Great Mosque), this is the centre of the picturesque bazaar area of little streets and fountains and a pedestrian precinct where it is pleasant to stroll. Silk cocoons are still sold in the Koza Han.
Open: Monday to Saturday, 9am–7pm.

ULUDAG
Turkey's premier ski resort, Uludag is one hour's drive from Bursa, or 30 minutes in the cable car (teleferik) which runs several times a day.

Çekirge

This is a hillside suburb 4km west of the town centre, where the spa baths are concentrated. The Baths of Eskikaplıca are the oldest and most interesting, dating from the 14th century.

Muradiye Cemetery

In the lovely grounds of the Muradiye mosque are the tombs of 12 early Ottomans, many with elaborately sculpted and painted wooden roofs.
In the western part of town best approached from Çekirge. Open: daily, 9am–noon and 3pm–6.30pm.

Tophane Park

This is the old citadel area above the Ulu Cami, where it is pleasant to sit on the terraces looking out over the town. The mausoleums of Osman, founder of the Ottoman empire, and his son Orhan Gazi, lie to the rear of the terraces.

Yeşil Camii and Türbe (Green Mosque and Mausoleum)

Bursa's principal monuments, they were built for Sultan Mehmed I between 1413 and 1421. They are famous for their magnificent tiled interiors.
Open: daily, 10am–noon and 2pm–5pm. Admission charge.

EDIRNE (ADRIANOPLE)

The only reason most people visit Edirne is to see the Selimiye Mosque, the building which Sinan himself always maintained was the culmination of his career. Built when he was 85 years old, Sinan brought together all his experience and research in Ottoman architecture to achieve this vast construction, its four minarets each over 70m tall.

Mimar Sinan Caddesi (town centre). A working mosque. Open: daily, except at prayer times.

GELIBOLU (GALLIPOLI)

This peninsula, where half a million soldiers lost their lives in World War I, is now a national park containing various war memorials. It was here in 1915 that the Allies mounted a disastrous expedition against the Turks who had joined forces with the Germans.

IZNIK (NICAEA)

Always associated with the tiles which were produced here from the 16th century onwards, the town today is visited mainly for its lakeside fish restaurants. Its Byzantine walls and ramparts are still well preserved.

MARMARA DENIZI (SEA OF MARMARA)

Ringed by green rolling hills, the Sea of Marmara boasts many beaches and resorts, the major ones of which are Mudanya, Gemlik and Yalova, all on the Asian or southern shore.

ISTANBUL ENVIRONS

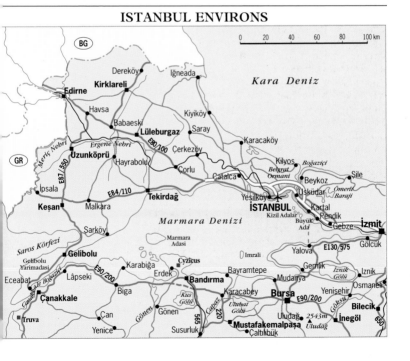

A Walk Around the Covered Bazaar

The Bazaar is open Monday to Saturday, 8.30am until 7pm. In wet weather it is the obvious choice for a visit, and you can stay here all day or just an hour as you like. The Bazaar, the largest in the world, has around 4,000 shops in total, employing some 30,000 people. Half a million people shop here every day. There are a dozen restaurants, several banks, numerous money-changers, teahouses and sandwich stalls, and it even has its own post office and police station.

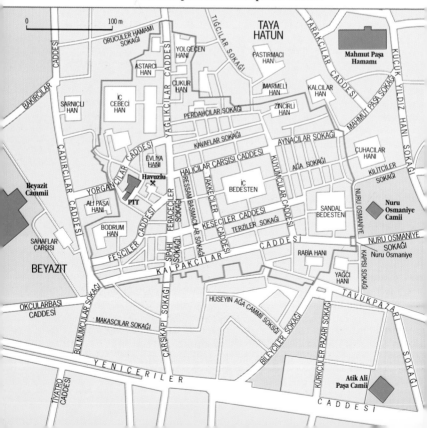

he best point of entry is the Nuru
smaniye Gate, also the most attractive
ie, which you can approach through the
recincts of the handsome Nuru Osmaniye
amii.

IRST IMPRESSIONS
nce inside, the first-time visitor will be
ruck by how clean and cheerful the
azaar is, with high airy ceilings and
vely tilework on many walls and
illars. The sheer quantity of goods is
verwhelming. On sale here are carpets,
labaster, antiques, ceramics, copper,
rass, gold and silver, leather, suede,
lothes, bags, shoes, backgammon sets,
ubble-bubble pipes, meerschaum
pes, hats, fezzes, woolly socks and
loves knitted by the nomads of Eastern
urkey – the list is endless.

The Bazaar was first established on
his site by Mehmet the Conqueror, and
as occupied much the same area ever
ince. He had it built even before his
alace and mosque, realising that the
riority was to bring vigorous
ommercial activity back into the
ecaying city. The Bazaar burns down
egularly. The last major fire was in
954 when it raged for three days.

Route planning as such never works, as the
isitor invariably gets lured off down a
empting sidestreet in no time. There are two
nes of approach. You can either just stick
 the main streets, making a short sortie to
he Iç Bedesten in the centre, or go right
und the edge, visiting all the hans where
ou can see many items being made, and
uy them too.

Ç BEDESTEN
ne place not to be missed is the Iç
Bedesten right in the middle, one of the
ew buildings that survives from the 15th

century, and where antiques, copper,
gold and silver jewellery are sold in an
area separated from the rest of the
Bazaar by four gateways with red
flashing lights over them. Also try to see
the Sandal Bedesteni, a 16th-century
hall where carpet auctions are held on
Mondays and Thursdays from 1pm
onwards, but pleasantly quiet at other
times.

ORIENTATION AND MERCHANDISE
Throughout the Bazaar the trades are all
grouped together as is the oriental
custom.The persistent touting is worst
in the main streets, but if you go deeper
into quieter side streets it tends to stop
altogether. Money can be changed
almost everywhere.
To watch silver items being made, and
even get something made or repaired
yourself, visit the Kalcılar Han in the
northeast corner. The nearby Zincirli
Han is also very attractive. For gold and
jewels, many shops are concentrated in
Kuyumcular Caddesi, between Sandal
Bedesteni and Iç Bedesten. The rug and
carpet merchants are clustered round
the Iç Bedesten. What is still called the
Fesciler Caddesi (Street of the
Fezmakers) now sells denim and blue
jeans.

For books, from maps to dictionaries
to novels in any language, new or
second-hand, go to the Sahaflar Çarşısı.
Lying strictly speaking just outside the
Bazaar, it is always crowded with
students from nearby Istanbul
University. The street that runs between
Sahaflar and the Bazaar itself is
Çadırcılar Caddesi, the Street of the
Tentmakers, a fascinating collection of
stores and workshops with prices often
cheaper than the Bazaar proper.

Sunset Walk from Pierre Loti's Café

This must be one of the most relaxing walks in Istanbul. It is all downhill or on the flat, and you are almost always away from the traffic – a most unusual phenomenon in Istanbul. For the full walk, incorporating all the sights *en route*, allow three hours. But even if you only have an hour to spare, it would still be enough to give you a feel for the magnificer Haliç (Golden Horn) and the Istanbul skyline.

Begin by taking a taxi to Pierre Loti's Café in the northern district Eyüp, a journey of about 20 minutes from the Blue Mosque area.

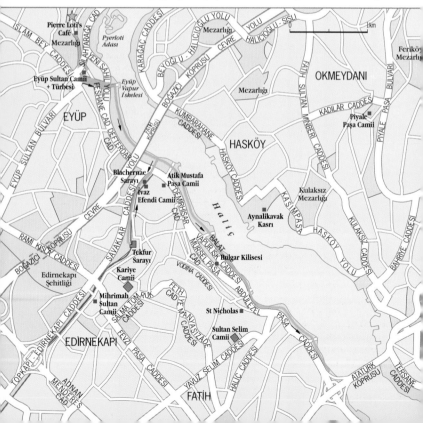

deally, aim to arrive about two hours before unset. The taxi bumps up the winding back reets to deposit you at the back of the café. erched on the edge of a steep drop, it verlooks the northern end of the Golden Iorn and below it sprawls the large, icturesque graveyard of Eyüp, the holiest arial ground in Istanbul.

PIERRE LOTI'S CAFÉ

'he café, named after the French ovelist who used to frequent it in the te 1800s, does not offer food but is a vonderful place for tea before the walk, vith dramatic views from the open erraces.

o start the walk, follow the wide stone path hat leads off down the hillside through the raveyard, admiring the elaborate mbstones of wealthy Ottomans along the ay. A leisurely descent takes about 15 inutes to the bottom.

Where the path meets the road, turn left hen first right to reach the entrance of the yüp Sultan Camii and Türbesi.

EYÜP SULTAN CAMII MOSQUE) AND EYÜP TÜRBESI TOMB)

This is the third holiest shrine in the Muslim world after Mecca and erusalem. Eyüp himself, standard-bearer and friend of the Prophet Muhammad, vas said to have been killed here during he first Arab siege of Constantinople in AD674. Except for the mosque, which vas rebuilt in 1798, the current complex f buildings dates from 1458. One of hese, the *imaret*, or soup kitchen, still erves some 500 local poor people at Iam each morning, the only one still unctioning in Istanbul.

Entering the attractive courtyard hrough the two main gateways, Eyüp's

tomb lies to the right. Leave your shoes outside, and step inside on to the carpets to admire the superb Iznik tiles covering the walls.

Leave the courtyard by the opposite gateway and turn left to walk through the old market street of Eyüp, where you may see mysterious twigs in bunches for sale. These are still used as toothbrushes by the poor, the wood becoming soft and pliable when moistened.

Continue in a straight line across the main road to reach the shore of the Golden Horn near the Eyüp Vapur Iskelesi (Eyüp landing stage).

3 HALIÇ (GOLDEN HORN)

Now that this Stamboul shoreline has been totally landscaped into parkland, it is a delight to stroll along the water's edge, well away from traffic noise, watching the distant minarets of the Süleymaniye and Ayasofya mosques get closer. The total distance from Eyüp to the Atatürk Köprüsü (Atatürk bridge) is 3.5km and you can complete the full length, looking at a few mosques and churches along the way, or break off at any time.

Walking under the motorway bridge, you soon come to the edge of the Byzantine land walls. A half-hour detour inland here takes the visitor to the ruined Palace of Blachernae and the Tekfur Sarayı (see pages 40–1). Fragments of the Byzantine sea walls run all along the Golden Horn to the Atatürk bridge.

Returning to the Golden Horn, the first mosque to look out for after about 500m is Atik Mustafa Paşa, a former 9th-century Byzantine church. Further on, you cannot fail to notice the painted metal church of St Stephen's of the Bulgars (see page 32). The walk ends at Atatürk bridge.

The Bosphorus By Boat

One of the most historic waterways of the world, this extraordinary winding strait that links the Black Sea to the Mediterranean is 32km long, with a width that fluctuates from 500m to 3km. Most organised cruises that run along it take half a day, but if you have time, turn it into a full day by getting off at the northernmost point of Anadolu Kavağı to have lunch, then hiring a taxi to take you back along the Asian shore, stopping off to visit the Küçüksu and Beylerbeyi palaces (see pages 40–1) on the Asian side, then crossing the Boğazıçı Köprüsü (old Bosphorus bridge) to be dropped off in the lovely Yıldız Park for a stroll and dinner on the Bosphorus.

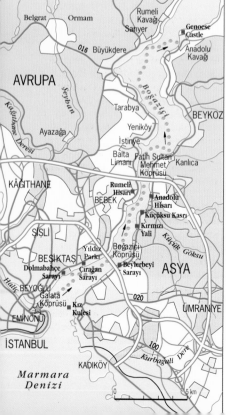

The public steamers which plough up and down the Bosphorus from the embarkation point at Eminönü by the Galata Köprüsü (Galata bridge), run frequently and are the equivalent of the local bus service. They have to be queued for in crowded halls and the boats themselves are rather shabby and squalid with limited on-deck seating. If you sit inside you do not get very good views, so it is preferable in the tourist season (mid-April to mid-October) to take the special tour boats which are much more luxurious and cruise much closer to the main sights.

The tour boats leave twice daily (morning and afternoon), from the Bosphorus Ferry Boat landing pier below the Topkapı about 400m from the Galata bridge.

THE FIRST LEG

When the boat sets off, it is best to focus initially on the views backwards towards the Topkapı and the mosque skyline. Then after gliding past the Dolmabahçe

Anadolu Kavağı, turn-round point for the river boats

Sarayı (see pages 40–1), the boat makes its first stop at Beşiktaş.

BEŞIKTAŞ TO KANLICA
Just beyond Beşiktaş is the vast restored waterfront palace, Çırağan Sarayı, which is now the Çırağan-Kempinksi Hotel (see page 40).

The eye is drawn next by the colossal 1973 Boğazıçı Köprüsü (Bosphorus bridge) and tucked just beyond it on the Asian side is the Beylerbeyi Sarayı (palace). When the 1987 bridge called Fatih Sultan Mehmet, the third longest suspension in the world, looms into view, you can spot, again on the Asian side, the splendid Kırmızı Yali, the Red Mansion, the best preserved seaside mansion on the Bosphorus, and about 500m further north towards the bridge, the little white palace of Küçüksu. Immediately beyond Küçüksu, just before the bridge, are two castles opposite each other, Rumeli Hisarı, on the European side and Anadolu Hisarı on the Asian side. This is the narrowest point of the Bosphorus, at a mere 500m, the same spot where the Persian king Darius chose to build his bridge of boats to transport his army across.

The boat stops at Kanlıca on the Asian side just after the bridge, and yogurt sellers usually embark to sell you the famous Kanlıca yogurt, eaten with a spoonful of sugar.

KANLICA TO SARIYER
Above the bridge, the districts on the European side are wealthy residential areas with many magnificent mansions on the shoreline. The district of Tarabya is famous for its many fish restaurants and the best hotel on the Bosphorus, the Büyük Tarabya.

The next stop is at Sarıyer, an attractive fishing village whose seafront is lined with tall houses in elaborate designs, some wooden, some brick, all in multitudinous colours.

THE FINAL LEG
From Sarıyer the boat crosses to the Asian side for the last stop at Anadolu Kavağı, where visitors can take their pick of the many fish restaurants. After lunch climb the hill to the Genoese castle on the summit for a fine sweeping view across the straits out to the so-called Clashing Rocks that mark the exit of the Black Sea, and which Jason and the Argonauts had to navigate on their search for the Golden Fleece.

The Aegean Region

*A*rguably Turkey's most beautiful region, the Aegean is an area of rolling hills and fertile valleys covered in cypress and pine trees, olive groves and vineyards. Even 2,500 years ago the famous historian Herodotus maintained it was blessed with the best climate in the world, and in summer there is always a gentle breeze to temper the summer heat. The coastline is magnificent, indented with endless bays and inlets. Some pockets are now heavily developed, but a coastline as long as this can never be fully built up and you never have to travel more than a few kilometres beyond the resorts to find deserted beaches and tiny fishing villages.

Maybe it was the beauty of these surroundings which encouraged the flowering here of brilliant civilisations, for after the fall of Troy around 1200BC several waves of Greek emigrants came and settled, founding cities which were soon well in advance of the Greek mainland, producing great scientists, historians and writers like Homer. The greatest of these ancient cities were Ephesus and Miletos, but throughout the Aegean region there are literally hundreds of ancient cities, the ruins of which can still be visited and explored.

AFRODISIAS (APHRODISIAS)

A generation ago this ruined Greek city was regarded as an attractive but

Aegean landscape

unexciting site, of interest primarily to archaeologists. All this was changed by one man, Professor Kenan Erim, who devoted his life to excavating the site, and his efforts have transformed the once buried ruins into a showpiece city that rivals Ephesus in its grandeur.

Two hours' drive from Kuşadası, Afrodisias is best reached by car or with an arranged tour, as it lies well off the main bus routes. Photography is forbidden in areas still under excavation. 166km inland from Kuşadası, off the Aydın–Denizli road. Open: daily, 8.30am–5.30pm. Admission charge.

Museum

Entry tickets to the site are bought here and you can admire the fine statues found on the site, many of Aphrodite herself, goddess of the city. She was originally an indigenous fertility goddess, only later becoming the Greek Olympian goddess of love and beauty. Aphrodisias was famous in antiquity for its school of sculpture, using the exquisite marble, often blue in colour, quarried from the local hills.

Theatre complex

The path from the museum leads first to the theatre, in front of which is an *agora* (market-place) with a magnificent

The Temple of Aphrodite in the ruined Greek city of Aphrodisias

colonnade of blue marble columns, with the large theatre baths beyond. Note especially the well-preserved carved seats in the front row of the theatre, for prominent people.

Baths of Hadrian and sports complex

The path leads over a hill and down to a plunge pool with a handsome black and white paved courtyard to one side, and the large Baths of Hadrian to the other. It was in this courtyard (*palaestra*) that sports and exercises would have been conducted.

Odeon and Bishop's Palace

Passing through the poplar-treed field which used to be the city's main market-place, you reach a charming little odeon (theatre) dating from the 2nd century AD, one of the most perfect structures of its kind in all Asia Minor. Beside it is the unusual building known as the Bishop's Palace, with a courtyard of lovely blue marble columns.

Temple of Aphrodite

The path leads on to the huge Temple of Aphrodite itself, thought to date from 100BC with many well-preserved Ionic columns still standing. In the late 5th century, the temple was converted to a Christian basilica.

Stadium

Beyond the temple lies the magnificent Stadium, one of the best preserved in the Greco-Roman world. Its 25 rows of seats had a capacity of 30,000, an indication of the flourishing population of the city.

Monumental gateway and Sebasteion

Returning in a loop back towards the museum, the path leads past the monumental gateway with its lovely spiral fluted columns, and on to the mysterious building called the Sebasteion, which encloses a processional way.

Gülets moored in Bodrum harbour, the ancient Greek port of Halicarnassus

BEHRAMKALE (ASSOS)

This fishing village with an attractive waterfront lies at the foot of an acropolis (a hilltop city centre) where the ruins of Assos stand facing out to sea. There is a small shingle beach, and it offers a few renovated old hotels which are popular with the artistic and literary community from Istanbul. On the approach to the village is a fine 14th-century Seljuk bridge. Ancient Assos has impressive fortified walls and the Temple of Athena, right on the summit, is the oldest Doric temple to have survived in Asia Minor.

93km south of Çanakkale, 73km south of Troy. Open: daily, 8.30am–5.30pm. Admission charge.

BODRUM (HALICARNASSUS)

Bodrum is one of the liveliest resorts in the Aegean, Turkey's San Tropez. There are people laughing and crowding the streets, colourful restaurants, pensions and cafés galore. Its atmosphere is more European Mediterranean than Turkish, and it has a certain ritziness in its bustle that is not found in most Turkish resorts. For entertainment and nightlife it takes some beating. A five-year building ban has now been imposed to prevent further development, which will ensure Bodrum's low-rise bohemian-style white bungalowed character remains unchanged.

Bodrum itself has no beaches and so a number of beach resorts have grown up on the peninsula beyond, such as Gümbet (the biggest), Turgutreis and Gümüşlük, all of which can easily use Bodrum as the lively centre.

Bodrum, ancient Halicarnassus, was famous in antiquity as the site of the Mausoleum, one of the Seven Wonders of the World. Nothing of this remains today beyond a few foundation blocks and a hole in the ground, but Bodrum is famed now instead for its role as the premier Aegean yachting centre, and for its fine Crusader castles.

Bodrum lies at the end of a peninsula, 174km south of Kuşadası, 195km north of Marmaris, three hours' drive from Izmir or three hours from Dalaman airport. Boats can be hired from the harbour for day trips to a whole range of deserted sandy coves, and to the Greek island of Kos opposite. For a land-based touring holiday, it is not ideal, as there is no escape from the hour-long drive up the peninsula to join the main coast road.

The ancient remains

Most of ancient Halicarnassus lies buried under the modern town and part of the charm of Bodrum today lies in stumbling across bits of ancient masonry set in the walls, used as door stops or lying about in gardens. Above the town, largely overgrown, is the ancient theatre which the energetic can climb up to for a fine view over the harbour. The famous Mausoleum, the magnificent tomb built by Queen Artemisia for her husband Mausolus in the 4th century BC, stood for 1,700 years and was finally destroyed by earthquakes. When the Crusader knights arrived in 1402 they used its remains as a quarry to build their castle. It lives on in this, and in the modern word it has given us.

Castle of St Peter

This is one of the last and finest examples of Crusader architecture in the east, magnificently preserved and in a spectacular setting on a promontory guarding the harbour.

The Knights Hospitaller of Rhodes built the castle around 1402 after the

Mongol leader Tamerlane destroyed their previous fortress in Izmir. But when Süleyman the Magnificent conquered their base on Rhodes in 1522, the knights were obliged to withdraw to Malta, abandoning the castle.

The castle is approached through a series of seven fortress gates and over a moat. Above the gates and scattered around inside look out for some fine carved relief blocks from the Mausoleum.

Inside is a museum showing finds from an ancient local shipwreck, and a total of five towers linked by escarpment walls. To explore the whole thing at leisure takes two hours, and an open-air café encourages lingering.

Open: daily, 9am–noon and 2pm–6pm. Admission charge.

Castle of St Peter, Bodrum

AEGEAN COAST

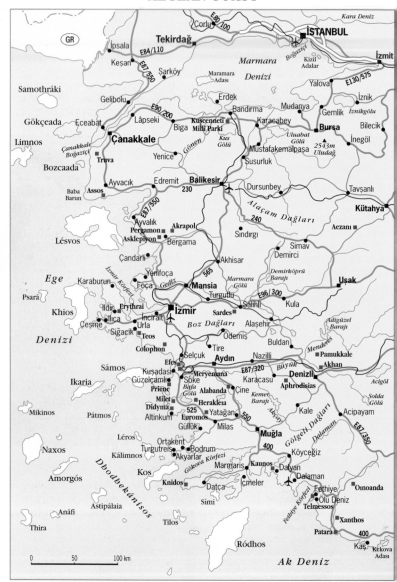

BIBLICAL TURKEY

The New Testament

Christianity took root very early in Asia Minor, with St Peter the Apostle founding the first Christian community in Antioch around AD47. It was here that the followers of Jesus were first called Christians, and the Acts of the Apostles describe how the disciples met for teaching, communal prayer and the breaking of bread. These were also the first congregations to include gentiles as well as Jews.

Ephesus became the principal centre of Christianity in Asia Minor in AD53, with the arrival of St Paul, who stayed for three years. He left, later to write his letters to the Ephesians, the most profound of his Epistles. St John the Apostle lived in Ephesus from AD37 to 48, accompanied, so many assert, by the Virgin Mary, whose tomb is claimed to be in the hills 7km south of Ephesus. John returned later still to write his gospel and died here in AD95.

The Old Testament

In Genesis, Mount Ararat is cited as the final resting place of Noah's Ark after the flood: 'And after the end of the hundred and fifty days the waters were abated. And the Ark rested on the seventh month, on the seventeenth day of the month, upon the mountains of Ararat'. Hopeful Christians make regular expeditions up the mountain in search of evidence for the existence of the ark, some claiming to have returned with pieces of it.

The biblical Ur of the Chaldees is the bustling modern town of Urfa (Sanliurfa), home of Abraham, before he was called 'to go forth into the land of Canaan'. He stopped off in Harran for several years until he was 75, and 1km northwest of Harran is a well known spot called Jacob's Well, Bir Yakub. Was it here that Jacob was said to have kissed Rachel and that Rebecca, later to marry Isaac, drew water for Abraham's servant?

DALAMAN

A small town where Dalaman airport, a former military airport, has been enlarged and converted to receive most of western Turkey's charter flights.

DALYAN (CAUNUS)

The fishing village of Dalyan, site of ancient Caunus, has been discovered in a big way recently, largely through the publicity of naturalist David Bellamy's Save the Loggerhead Turtle campaign. It has burgeoned into a bustling place with many hotels, and tourists are asked to swim from the other end of the long beach to avoid damage to turtle eggs.

A visit to ancient Caunus, however, remains a special experience, reachable only by boat from the promenade.

From the disembarkation point, the path takes you up past the ruins of a Byzantine basilica and a huge Roman bath, now converted to a museum. At the foot of the acropolis hill, crowned by the ruins of a 4th-century BC fortress, lies the Greek-style theatre.

Downriver, you can take a boat to the mud baths and sulphur springs. *Dalyan lies 10km off a side road from the main Marmaris–Fethiye road, south of Lake Köyceğiz. Open: daily, 8.30am–5.30pm. No admission charge as such, but the site has to be reached by boat and the boatman's fee is negotiable.*

Efes (Ephesus)

Showpiece of the Aegean, Ephesus today is visited daily by thousands. Sacred city of Artemis, famous throughout history for its temple which was one of the Seven Wonders of the World, Ephesus also boasts many magnificent Roman remains from the time when it was capital of the Roman province of Asia.

Ephesus is one of the largest archaeological sites in the world and falls into three distinct areas: the Artemision (site of the Temple of Artemis); the old acropolis with the Byzantine fortress and St John's basilica; and finally the city of Ephesus itself, about 2km away.

Ephesus is a 45-minute drive from Izmir. It lies 17km north of Kuşadası on the road to Selçuk. Open: daily, 8.30am–sunset. Admission charge.

Temple of Artemis

The approach is marked by yellow signs from the village of Selçuk. The greatest temple in all Asia Minor, originally four times greater in area than the Parthenon in Athens, it had 127 columns, each nearly 20m high. Artemis of the Ephesians was a Greek adaptation of the Anatolian earth-mother, whose outstanding quality was her fertility, depicted in her statues by the bulls' testicles hanging from her chest, a sacrifice that would have been offered to her annually. On her annual feast day, orgies were held here. The cult was continued by the Romans, identifying her with their own fertility goddess Diana, and the temple was the object of pilgrimage for more than 1,000 years, conferring great wealth on the city. The solitary temple column that rises today from a muddy pool is a challenge to most visitors' powers of imagination.

Christianity in Ephesus

The goddess's downfall was the advent of Christianity which came early to Ephesus. St Paul lived and preached here, later writing his Epistles to the Ephesians. St John, accompanied according to tradition by the Virgin Mary, wrote his Gospel in Ephesus and died here in AD95. His tomb lies in the vast Basilica of St John.

The main Ephesus site

Though not blessed with a spectacular setting like Pergamum or Priene, Ephesus' unique interest lies in its completeness as a city. Walking along its

The magnificent façade of the Library of Celsus

The colossal centre-stage of Ephesus' Roman theatre

magnificent white marble streets flanked with colonnades, shops, civic buildings and the houses of the wealthy, it is perhaps easier here than in any other Greco-Roman city to relive its past grandeurs.

Theatre

From the site entrance, head straight for the theatre and climb to the top seats for an overview of the city. Most of the ruins that lie before you date from the Roman imperial age, when the population was about 250,000. The seating capacity of the theatre is 25,000, and it is still used for performances during the annual Selçuk Festival (see pages 158–9). St Paul preached here, and the acoustics today are as excellent as they were then.

Library of Celsus

Standing at the end of the Marble Street, this library is the best-preserved structure of its kind, named after Celsus, Proconsul of Asia in AD106, and whose tomb is inside it. Behind the library is the massive Temple of Serapis, part of the Egyptian bull cult.

Downtown Ephesus

Beyond the library the street which snakes uphill (Curetes Street) leads into what is regarded as downtown Ephesus, with wealthy Roman apartments to the right and public buildings to the left. Do not miss the communal latrines in this left area, and the private houses also merit closer inspection for their murals and mosaics.

IZMIR (SMYRNA)

One of the chief pleasures of holidaying along the Aegean and Mediterranean coasts is that the places of interest and the ancient sites do not tend to lie in the cities, but rather in small villages, on beaches, or in the middle of the countryside. Visitors are therefore only rarely obliged to stay in a city to see the sights. This is certainly true of Izmir, Turkey's third largest city, a cosmopolitan port with a turbulent past.

If you do pass through the centre rather than use the new bypass, look out for the Kadifekale, the flat-topped hill that was the ancient acropolis, and the Roman agora (open: daily, 8.30am–5.30pm). The harbourfront offers a host of excellent fish restaurants with delicacies like sea bass and lobster. The colourful Ottoman bazaar area is just inland from the clock tower.

Ancient Greek Smyrna is now modern Izmir

IZMIR ENVIRONS

Çeşme

The most famous of the beach resorts around Izmir, Çeşme is a well-established resort and thermal spa with long sheltered sandy beaches, several holiday villages and the full range of watersports. It is an attractive fishing town with a relaxed atmosphere, and the harbour is dominated by a splendid 14th-century Genoese fortress. Behind the fortress is a labyrinth of twisting backstreets, and along the promenade are myriad seafront restaurants of varying quality.

The excellent beaches lie a little outside the town, but are easily accessible by taxi or *dolmus* (shared taxi running on a regular route).

A ferry runs twice weekly to the Greek island of Chios (Khios) 14km offshore. The journey takes one hour.

80km west of Izmir, 90 minutes' drive from Izmir airport.

Çesme harbour front with fishing boats. The town is famed for its thermal baths

Foça

This pretty fishing village with its cobbled streets and whitewashed houses is still a very Turkish place with just a few hotels beside the beach. The Club Med has a holiday village near by.

45km northwest of Izmir, 50 minutes' drive from Izmir airport.

Gümüldür

A small resort on a long sandy beach, safe for children, offering watersports.

35km north of Kuşadası, 45km south of Izmir.

Sart (Sardes)

A rarely visited but very worthwhile place, Sardes was the ancient capital of the Lydian Empire under King Croesus, he of the legendary wealth. The recently excavated ruins are very impressive.

90km east of Izmir on the E23 to Uşak.

Open: daily, 8.30am–5.30pm. Admission charge.

Sigacık

This seaside village is a pretty spot with a fine Genoese fortress dominating its harbour. On the headland 2km beyond it are some lovely sheltered bays with camping and hotels. The ancient site of Teos lies near by in the olive groves.

45km southwest of Izmir

SMYRNA'S WINE

Ancient Smyrna was famous for its wine, which Homer tells us was drunk sweet and mixed with honey, chalk and powdered marble. On top of this, it was diluted five parts to two with water. To drink wine neat was considered quite barbaric.

ALEXANDER: THE GREEK

The arrival of Alexander the Great on the ancient scene opened a new era in history, and especially for Turkey. At the tender age of 21 Alexander crossed the Hellespont in 334BC at the head of an army of about 35,000 Macedonians and Greeks, with the express goal of liberating the Greek cities and conquering the Persian Empire. He achieved his aim with remarkable speed, encountering the mysterious Gordion knot on the way (Gordion lies 106km west of Ankara). This was the knot that the Phrygian king had tied to fix the yoke to the pole of his ox-cart, and an oracle had foretold that whoever undid it would be master of Asia. Having heard of the legend, Alexander felt obliged to fulfil the prophecy. He took one look and simply sliced the knot through with his sword. Within 18 months he had

TURKEY

Alexander dressed for battle

Below: detail of the Alexander Sarcophagus, Istanbul Archaeological Museum

Far left: the ruined stadium at Perge

retaken Anatolia and within three years had conquered the entire Persian Empire.

When Alexander died in Babylon at 32 from a sudden fever, his vast, newly acquired empire was left without an heir. His generals proceeded to squabble among themselves for 20 years and finally three main kingdoms emerged: the Macedonians in Greece, the Seleucids in Syria and the Ptolemies in Egypt.

His conquest, however, created a corridor linking Greece to Persia and the east, a corridor down which ideas could travel and cross-fertilise, sowing the seeds for a tremendous flowering of thought and scholastic achievement that was to transform the civilised world. It was known as the Hellenistic period and lasted 1,000 years.

Planned to be the eighth Wonder of the World, the Temple of Apollo at Didyma was never fully completed. Wars and a shortage of money interrupted construction

KUŞADASI (BIRD ISLAND)

Trebled in size in the last 10 years, Kuşadası is now Aegean Turkey's major resort, a bustling town set in a wide bay. What it offers is a lively centre for entertainment and nightlife, and a good location as a base for excursions, notably to nearby Ephesus.

Its name comes from the island at the end of the bay, now linked to the mainland by a concrete causeway. The Genoese fortress on the island still guards the harbour. Besides its yacht marina, Kuşadası is also a port of call for Aegean cruise ships, and boats run daily to the Greek island of Sámos opposite.

There is a small public beach on the main bay, but the sandy beach at Kadınlar Plajı (Ladies' Beach) 3km from the centre is preferable. The lively bazaar offers a fine selection of jewellery and clothing, and there are more restaurants clustered together in the town and seafront than you could ever sample. *94km south of Izmir, 17km southwest of Ephesus, 174km north of Bodrum. On the coast opposite Sámos. Ninety minutes transfer to Izmir airport.*

KUŞADASI ENVIRONS

Didyma

Associated above all with its magnificent Medusa heads, Didyma is the name of the great temple precinct of Apollo's oracle, famous throughout antiquity for its predictions. The oracle itself was located in the innermost chamber of the temple, tended by the chief priest and the priestesses. Christianity spelt the end of the oracle racket. Emperor Theodosius announced in AD385: 'No

ortal man shall have the effrontery to
ncourage vain hopes by the inspection of
ntrails, or which is worse, to attempt to
arn the future by the detestable
onsultation of oracles'.

*km north of Altınkum (a small but growing
sort with a sandy beach) and 72km south
f Ephesus. Open: daily, 8.30am–5.30pm.
dmission charge.*

phesus, see pages 62–3.

ilet (Miletos)

great ancient sea-trading city that
valled Ephesus at its peak, Miletos is
ell worth a visit. Its prosperity was
ased on its four sheltered harbours,
ifficult to imagine now, as the sea is 8km
way as a result of the Maeander river
alley silting up. The process is on-going,
nd the Aegean is getting further away at
he staggering rate of 6m a year. The site
s extensive, and the major monument is
he theatre, perhaps the most outstanding
Greco-Roman theatre in Turkey. There
re more than 200 Greek or Roman
heatres in Turkey. Look out as well for
he Roman Baths of Faustina, with walls
till over 15m high.

*3km south of Kuşadası, 133km north of
Bodrum, 26km south of Priene and 19km
orth of Didyma. Open: daily,
.30am–sunset. Admission charge.*

Priene

Reminiscent in some ways of a miniature
Delphi, the ancient city of Priene is very
Greek, with none of the grandiose Roman
monuments that abound elsewhere. It
oasts a spectacular setting perched up in
he lee of a vast rock outcrop. As a small
Greek town it contrasts well with the
grandeur of Roman Ephesus. Like
Miletos, Priene was once on the sea, but
s now more than 15km away.

The vast Roman theatre at Miletos

Note the interesting quarter of
private houses, and a charming Greek
theatre now shaded by pine trees. From
here a path leads up the rocky outcrop
to the sanctuary of Demeter from where
there are superb views.
*26km north of Miletos, 42km south of
Kuşadası and 44km north of Didyma.
Open: 8.30am–sunset. Admission charge.*

Byzantine castle atop Miletos theatre

Marmaris harbour front

MARMARIS

Set in a huge fjord-like bay with pine forests reaching right down to the sea, Marmaris is one of Turkey's most attractive resorts. After Bodrum, Marmaris is the Aegean's main yachting centre and embarkation point for boating holidays, but it retains a much more Turkish feel to it than Bodrum.

The harbour promenade is enjoyable for strolling and the older part of the town, with its excellent bazaar, is a pedestrian precinct lined with colourful restaurants and cafés. Unlike Bodrum, Marmaris has a good town beach but to find secluded swimming you can take a *dolmus* or a water taxi to numerous pretty bays near by. Most of the larger hotels are situated in İçmeler (8km to the west), with its fine shingle beach kept immaculately clean, or at Turunç (9km to the south), again with a safe, sandy bay. Both places are linked to Marmaris by a cheap and regular water taxi.
Marmaris is a 90-minute drive from Dalaman airport, on a peninsula 61km south from Muğla, off the main Muğla-Dalaman road.
Boats run daily to Ródhos (Rhodes), directly opposite the Gulf of Marmaris, taking between two and three hours each way depending on the size of the boat.

MARMARIS ENVIRONS

Datça
A small fishing village that has grown to resort and was once the site of old Cnidos.
75km west of Marmaris.

Knidos (Cnidos)
Right at the tip of the peninsula, Cnidos can be a day's outing by boat or by car. has attractive Greco-Roman ruins in a fine setting on a headland, and offers swimming and some simple fish restaurants.
107km west from Marmaris. Open: daily, 8.30am–sunset. Admission charge.

MILAS

Set in a fertile plain surrounded by wooded mountains, Milas (ancient Mylasa) is a busy town on a natural crossroads, its river banks lined with once lovely but now decaying Ottoman mansions. Before the Ottomans, the local dynasty called the Menteşe emirs ruled here from their castle stronghold Peçin Kale, visible from miles around on the dramatic flat-topped mountain just south of Milas. This splendid fortress was in use by the local governor until the 17th century, and can still be visited today.
72km northeast of Bodrum, 131km northwest of Marmaris and 71km west of Muğla. Open: daily, 8.30am–6pm. Admission charge.

MILAS ENVIRONS

Bafa Gölü (Lake Bafa)
This beautiful lake makes a good stopping place for lunch on day trips in the area, with its simple lakeside fish restaurants. The evocative ruins of ancient Herakleia lie on the opposite

Sanctuary of Zeus at Labranda

shore, approachable by a small track.
30km northwest of Milas.

Euromos

You cannot miss the elegant columns of
this temple by the roadside. It dates
from the 2nd century AD and is one of
Asia Minor's best preserved temples.
*15km north of Milas on the way to Lake
Bafa. Open: daily, 8.30am–6pm.
Admission charge.*

Labranda

Set high in the hills above Milas, this is
the site of a sanctuary to Zeus, originally
joined to ancient Mylasa by a paved
sacred way. It is an impressive site, well
excavated by the Swedes since 1969.
*17km north of Milas. Open: daily,
8.30am–6pm. Admission charge.*

MUĞLA

Set up on a plateau at 680m the town of
Muğla is the capital of Muğla Province
and was also the capital of the Menteşe
emirs in the 16th century. The old
quarter lies to the north of the main
road and it makes a pleasant change
from all the Greco-Roman sites to
wander in the bazaar and into the
winding lanes with their attractive
Ottoman houses.
*135km east of Bodrum, 73km north of
Marmaris.*

MUĞLA ENVIRONS

Alinda (Karpuzlu) and Alabanda

A visit to these two ruined cities makes
an interesting day trip, away from the
beaches, in the depths of rural Turkey.
Alinda is remarkably well preserved, in
spite of never having been excavated,
with the finest Greek market building in
the country.
60km north of Muğla on the road to Aydın.

Bathers at Pamukkale's Turizm Motel

PAMUKKALE

Even though the spot is now highly commercialised, Pamukkale is a unique natural wonder and will leave an unforgettable impression. A bizarre network of fantastical open-air white stalactite rock formations and hot springs, its name means 'Cotton Castle', a graphic description of the white terraces tumbling down the hillside. The limestone deposits in the water are continuously building on to the structure, and it has taken 14,000 years for them to reach their current state.

Turks themselves, always keen on natural wonders, are very fond of the place, and it is a popular day's outing from far around. Stalls selling cheap souvenirs abound and the atmosphere is always festive. The big hotels have enclosed the major rock pools within their grounds, and the two best are

reckoned to be that of the Tusan Motel, with two deep interconnecting pools, and the Turizm Motel whose pool is still full of Roman capitals and columns to bump your shins on.

As a visitor it is *de rigueur* to shed your shoes and wade about in as many rock pools as you can find, or if you get totally carried away, to submerge yourself and wallow hippo-like in the warm water. The waters are claimed to benefit heart and circulation complaints, as well as digestive, rheumatic and kidney diseases.

Pamukkale's hot springs were credited from the first with religious and mystical qualities, so early cities grew up here centred round the springs. The ancient city that is still in evidence behind the Cotton Castle is called Hierapolis, Holy City, dating from Roman times.

If you are fortunate enough to be spending the night at Pamukkale, it is pleasant to stroll round the extensive remains at dusk or even by moonlight. The vaulted baths have been turned into a museum and this is the only part of the site that has opening hours (9am–5pm) and an admission charge.

The major monument in terms of size is the large Roman theatre with its well-preserved stage building. Beyond this, the road leads out through the monumental northern gateway to reach the vast necropolis, one of the most extensive in all Asia Minor. Over 1,200 sarcophagi have been counted, all lining the beginning of the ancient route to Ephesus.

217km west of Kuşadası, off the main E24 road, and 17km north of Denizli.
Pamukkale is a three-hour drive from Kuşadası. The whole area never shuts and there is no admission charge to the main site.

Above: sunset paddling at Pamukkale

Right: colours of the rainbow in Pamukkale's rock formations

PAMUKKALE ENVIRONS

Akhan

Just 1km after the turn-off to Pamukkale on the road east towards Dinar stands an impressive Seljuk *caravanserai* faced in pinkish marble, traditional overnight accommodation for travelling merchants. There are at least 50 of these handsome Seljuk *hans* on the main trade routes of central Anatolia, all built in the 13th century when the Seljuk Turks were the dominant power in Anatolia.

TURKISH CARPETS

Carpet weaving is a great Turkish art introduced by the nomadic Seljuks in the 12th century. Their art recalled their nomadic background, for the carpet is the essential piece of tent furniture.

There are three categories of rug: the knotted pile carpets (*hali*), flat weaves (*kilim*) characterised by their lack of pile and their rug-like size, and the silks, which are in a class of their own. These are the most expensive and the most luxurious, and the fineness of the silk yarn allows the weaver to create minute detail in the rich colours. *Kilims* were traditionally made by women for use at home, not for sale. Patterns and colours were therefore not dictated by commercial expediency but were reflections of the weaver's identity, her family and her tribe. Most *kilims* are sheep's wool, but some are goat hair and cotton. In the home they were used as floor covering but also as wall hangings, door curtains, prayer rugs, large bags for cushions and saddlebags, and small bags for salt, bread, grain or clothing.

Natural dyes were traditionally made from roots, bark, berries, vegetables and minerals. Then in the second half of the 19th century aniline chemical dyes were discovered and

their use has gradually replaced most of the old vegetable dyes. Pink and orange were never found in natural substances, so the presence of these or any other colour with a harsher brightness indicates chemical dyes. Today's weavers invariably use chemical dyes for convenience, and have therefore been freed from the constraints of plant availability in their area which in the past

Far left, above and below: Anatolian women plying their skills. Above and below: displayed wares in the Covered Bazaar, Istanbul

led to certain dominant colours in certain areas, such as Turcoman red and Balıkesir blue and red. The designs and patterns also give clues to the region, though it takes years of practice to identify carpets correctly. A few designs are common to all areas, notably the prayer rug with its solid arch-shaped block of colour representing the *mihrab* (prayer niche) that faces Mecca in a mosque wall. Prayer rugs were used exclusively for prayer and the range of symbols to look out for on them are the hands of prayer, the mosque lamp, the tree of life, the water jug, the jewel of Muhammad or the star of Abraham.

PERGAMUM

One of Turkey's most impressive sites by virtue of its striking setting on a steep acropolis. At its peak in the second century BC, Pergamum rivalled Alexandria as a centre of learning and science, with a famous library building the remnants of which can still be seen on the acropolis. In an act of eccentricity, the last Pergamum king bequeathed his entire kingdom to Rome, thus hastening the advent of Roman influence in Asia Minor.

Pergamum is adjacent to the Turkish town of Bergama, 3km off the E24 coast road from Çanakkale to Izmir. It is 197km north of Izmir and 243km south of Çanakkale. Site open: daily, 8.30am–5.30pm. Admission charge. Archaeological Museum open: Tuesday to Sunday, 9am–noon and 1.30pm–5pm.

Acropolis and theatre

German archaeologists have reconstructed many of the buildings on this fine citadel, including five kings' palaces, the famous library and the temple of Athena, patroness of learning. The Pergamum library was said to have contained 200,000 books, written for the first time on animal skins, known as 'pergamum paper', from which the English word parchment comes. Mark Antony, to please Cleopatra, presented the entire Pergamene library to Alexandria, where books had always been written on papyrus. The theatre, built into the steep hillside, is a remarkable piece of Hellenistic engineering.

The citadel at Pergamum was eventually destroyed in the 15th century by the Mongols

Asklepieion

Set down below the acropolis are the remains of a remarkable medical centre dedicated to Asklepius, god of healing. This popular centre was based upon the fame of Galen, the greatest physician of late antiquity, born here in AD129. Some patients stayed here as long as a year. One Roman patient, suffering from indigestion, was put on a diet of bread and cheese with parsley and lettuce, told to go barefoot and take a run each day, to coat himself with mud and anoint himself with wine before entering a hot bath. A grateful inscription tells us his treatment was successful.

Red Basilica

In the old Turkish quarter of Bergama stands this colossal red-brick Byzantine basilica, originally a Roman temple to the Egyptian bull god of Serapis. A fine Roman three-arched bridge spans the river near by.

TRUVA (TROY)

Troy is a city that lives in the imagination through Homer's tales in the *Iliad* and the *Odyssey*. To find that it really exists comes as a surprise to many, but far from being the mighty city of Helen and King Priam, it is today a series of shapeless mounds and ditches with occasional outcrops of wall and foundation. In an attempt to make up for the lack of exciting remains, the authorities have constructed an enormous wooden horse at the site entrance. Children can climb up inside this to relive the legendary climax of the siege of Troy when the Greeks tricked their way inside the city walls.

Heinrich Schliemann was the German businessman and amateur archaeologist whose romantic childhood

A reconstruction of the fabled Wooden Horse, the downfall of an unsuspecting Troy

obsession with Troy first led to its rediscovery. He obtained permission from the Ottoman sultan to excavate here in 1870, using money he had amassed in the California goldrush, and spent the next 20 years of his life pursuing his dream. He was rewarded with the discovery of four Troys, one on top of the other, and the so-called Jewels of Helen, in which his wife posed for newspapers and which Schliemann kept until bequeathing them to the Berlin Museum.

Today there are thought to have been a total of nine Troys, layer upon layer. Which one was Homer's Troy is the subject of a modern Trojan war, with Troy VI and Troy VII as the main contenders.

As you walk round the small site, all the various levels are labelled, but the whole nevertheless comes across as very confusing.

5km off the E24 coast road between Çanakkale and Ayvacık and 32km southwest of Çanakkale. Open: 8.30am–5.30pm. Admission charge.

A Walk to Gerga

Gerga is a tiny remote site which you will not find marked on many maps. It is a rarely visited and little known hilltop settlement and makes an exciting day trip from Kuşadası, Bodrum or Marmaris, involving about 90 minutes' drive each way and up to three hours' walking. It is approached by drivable track from Eskiçine, and then on foot for the final 3km. Eskiçine lies equidistant between Aydin to the north and Muğla to the south. It is best to go armed with your own provisions as there are scant eating facilities in the area, yet many lovely picnic sites.

The rugged landscape offers a complete contrast from the coast, with a few hamlets being the only habitation in the vicinity of Gerga itself. The hilltop ruins are unique in Turkey as an example of an early indigenous town, untouched by Hellenisation or Romanisation, utterly different from the sophisticated coastal cities like Ephesus and Priene.

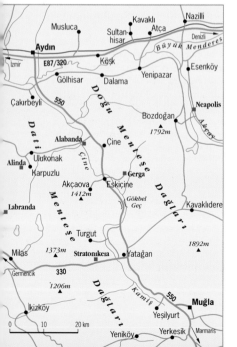

Driving north from Muğla, pass through Yatağan where the approach road leads through a pretty gorge with weird canyon-like formations of rock toadstools and cones.

ÇINE GORGE

The Çine river which runs through the gorge flows strongly even in the summer months, and at the point where the gorge ends, a beautiful old bridge spans the river. Built for pedestrians only, its narrow walkway is still in perfect condition. There is meant to be a path from this bridge up to Gerga in an hour's walk, but it is hard to find without a guide.

Driving on to Eskiçine past the Seljuk mosque on the right, look out for a drivable track off to the right which leads, after about 4km, to the village of Ovacık. From here the track winds on for a further 7 or 8km to reach the village of Kırksakallar

The extraordinary miniature temple at Gerga

Forty Beards).

Parking next to the neat white school building at Kırksakallar, the walk from here across the ridges to Gerga takes the best part of an hour. Follow the charming walled path that leads out beyond the village between the fields and when it stops, just keep going in the same direction, dipping down one moment, climbing another.

After half an hour watch out for a large rock in the form of a toadstool, incribed with huge letters in Greek, GERGA. In the approach from now on, you will see several such ancient signposts directing the way.

GERGA

The modern Turkish name for Gerga is Gâvurdamları, meaning infidel-roofed-sheds, a curious reference to the strange architecture of Gerga, where the tiny stone buildings are remarkable for their well-formed roofs. Descending a ridge in a westerly direction the first stone-roofed hut can be made out on the hillside opposite. Two lions' heads jut out from the blocks just below the roof. Beyond, further along the shady terrace, lies the building for which Gerga is justly renowned, an endearing little temple, scarcely 5m cubed, with a gabled roof of stone, carved with the letters GERGA again. The other relics of the town include various fallen cult statues, some curious stone obelisks and wine presses, all scattered about the lovely manmade terraces, impressively shored-up with rock walls and buttresses.

Mediterranean Turkey

*T*urkey's southern shore has to rank as one of the most beautiful stretches of coastline anywhere in the Mediterranean. Known as the Turquoise Coast or the Turkish Riviera, it stretches for some 600km from Fethiye right through to Iskenderun near the Syrian border. The coastline falls into several distinct regions, so varied that as you pass from one to the other it is almost like entering a different country. The whole length, however, shares the benefit of an excellent climate with 300 days of sunshine a year.

The first region, from Fethiye to Kemer, is called Lycia, with the wildest and most dramatic coastal scenery in Turkey. The mountains tumble right down to the sea and there are glorious sandy beaches and spectacular ruined cities to explore.

The next region, from Antalya to Side, is Pamphylia, a flat fertile coastal plain with the mountains set further back from the sea.

From Alanya, the region that extends to the Syrian border is called Cilicia, the western section of which runs round the headland to Silifke and is rugged and beautiful but sparsely populated. The coastal drive is magnificent but tiring. The Cilician plain from Mersin to Iskenderun is the least interesting stretch of Turkey's Mediterranean coast, with flat river valleys and industrial sprawl round the city of Adana.

ADANA

Set on the banks of the Seyhan river, Adana, Turkey's fourth largest city after Istanbul, Ankara and Izmir, is the centre of a rich agricultural region and of the prosperous cotton industry. Besides its 16-arch Roman bridge and its covered bazaar, the only other building of significance is the Ulu Cami (Great Mosque) built in 1507 from black and white marble. It lies on Abidin Paşa Caddesi in the city centre, quite close to the Roman bridge. The city has several good hotels and makes a good base for visiting nearby sites.

ADANA ENVIRONS

Dilekkaya (Anavarza)

The ruins of this lovely Roman Byzantine city include a stadium, tombs, an aqueduct, a theatre and several basilicas. *30km north from Ceyhan, 72km northeast from Adana. Open: always. Admission free*

Karatepe

A striking Hittite site in the mountains with many fine sculptures still *in situ*. *77km north from Ceyhan, 129km northeast from Adana. Open: daily, 8.30am–5.30pm. Admission charge.*

> **FERRIES TO NORTHERN CYPRUS**
> Car ferries run from Mersin to
> Gazimagusa (Famagusta) and from
> Tasucu to Girne (Kyrenia) in North
> Cyprus. A hydrofoil service for
> passengers also runs to Girne. Fares
> are cheap and tickets can be bought
> at the docks without advance
> booking. (See Boat Trips, pages
> 140–1.)

Kızkalesi (Maiden's Castle)

A 12th-century Armenian castle 100m
offshore, with fine beaches near by. It is
difficult to visit.
122km southwest from Adana on the E24.

Mersin

Originally a Hittite city, one of the oldest
continuously inhabited places in the
world, there is little to see today.
67km west of Adana on the E24.

Slifke

A pleasant town on the banks of the
Göksu river overlooked by the Crusader
castle on its acropolis, from which there
are fine views. A 15-minute drive further

east are the curious caves of Cennet and
Cehennem (Heaven and Hell).
161km southwest from Adana on the E24.

Tarsus

A charming town with old houses and
gardens, famous as the place where
Antony first met Cleopatra, and the
birthplace of St Paul. His pre-Christian
name was Saul of Tarsus.
42km west of Adana on the E5.

Uzuncaburç (Diocaesarea)

A pretty village surrounded by the
Roman ruins of a theatre, some temples
and a tall Hellenistic tower.
38km north of Silifke.

Yakapinar (Misis)

The site of superb Roman mosaics,
notably of Noah's Ark and the Flood.
*28km east of Adana. Open: daily,
9am–5pm. Admission charge.*

Yılanlıkale (Castle of the Snake)

An imposing eight-towered, 13th-
century Armenian castle.
*6km east of Ceyhan on the road to
Gaziantep, 48km east of Adana. Open:
always. Admission free.*

MEDITERRANEAN COAST

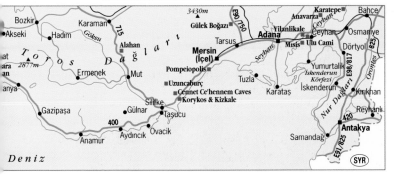

ALANYA

A modern beach resort and ancient Seljuk city, Alanya's prominent feature is its mighty rock which juts out Gibraltar-like into the sea. On top is its amazing red-brick crenellated fortress (red bricks were the favoured building material of the Seljuks), and below on either side are sandy beaches with the modern town and its hotels.

The fortress with its 150 towers enclosed the 13th-century town built by the Seljuk sultan Keykubad I, who used it as his winter quarters and naval base. The outer wall is 7km long and took 12 years to build. The walk up from the modern town takes about 40 minutes, so

Exploring the Damlatas caves at the foot of the Alanya rock citadel

many may prefer to take a taxi, especially on a hot summer's day. Within the walls you can explore old gateways, Byzantine chapels, the dilapidated residential quarter, mosques, a *bedestan* (covered market) and *caravanserai* and the citadel at the very summit.

In the old Seljuk dockyard area below the rock stands the colossal Kızıl Kule (Red Tower) built to defend the port. From this port area you can hire small boats to explore the many grottoes which honeycomb the base of the Alanya rock. *131km east of Antalya on the E24. Open: always. Admission free.*

ANAMUR

The rugged landscape all around the headland of Anamur was notorious for piracy and brigandage in ancient times, and many ruined fortresses litter the coast. The best preserved and largest of these is Anamur, a Crusader castle with all its walls and 36 towers still standing. Right on the beach with the waves lapping its walls, it dominates the surrounding plain and was the foothold on the mainland for the Lusignan kings of Cyprus, which is less than 80km away. Inside you can climb stairways up many of the towers. Two kilometres west of the castle the ruins of a Byzantine city called Anemurium cover the hillside, with traces of mosaic and painting in the private houses (it is always open to the public, admission free). *3km east of Anamur town on the E24. Anamur castle is open: daily, 8.30am–5.30pm. Admission charge.*

ANTAKYA (ANTIOCH)

Until 1939 Antakya and this curious pocket of land known as the Hatay in the southeast corner of the Mediterranean

Anamur Kalesi, the 11th-century Crusader castle at Anamur

belonged to Syria, but the French gave it to Turkey in exchange for support against Germany in World War II. Set in pleasantly hilly countryside, Antakya lies on the Orontes river. In Roman times, as ancient Antioch, it was a notorious centre of good living, not to say depravity, and it is the remnants from those days that make the town worth visiting today. These take the form of Roman mosaics from the floors of private houses, the finest collection in the world. Dating from the second and third centuries AD, they are displayed in the Hatay Archaeological Museum (open: Tuesday to Sunday, 8.30am–noon and 1.30pm–5pm, admission charge). Besides the museums, the town has an old Roman bridge over the river and a picturesque bazaar quarter.

193km southeast of Adana on the E5, 104km west of Aleppo.

ANTAKYA ENVIRONS

Harbiye (Daphne)

This was Antioch's pleasure suburb where most of the lavish villas were situated, and where Apollo's pursuit of the nymph Daphne is said to have taken place. The laurel into which she turned herself still grows all around. Nothing remains of the buildings, but the gardens and streams are still a popular weekend picnic site for the modern residents of Antakya.

Samandağ

From Antakya it is a 30-minute drive to the beautiful sandy beach, near which are the ruins of Seleucia Persia, the ancient port of Antioch, once one of the greatest ports in the Mediterranean.

ALARA HAN

About 39km along the main coast road from Alanya a sign points inland to Alara Han, an unusual Seljuk *caravanserai* with a richly carved main door. This *han* (an inn for travelling merchants) is one of seven along the road from Konya and Alanya, standing a day's walk apart from each other. On the hilltop north of it stands the breathtaking Seljuk fortress, reached by a tunnel, where travellers would take refuge if attacked by bandits. It takes a good hour to climb to the summit. (Open: always. Admission free.)

Built by Romans, the Aspendos theatre can seat 15,000. The city declined when the harbour silted up

ANTALYA

This is the major resort of Mediterranean Turkey, a city rather than a town, with its own airport and industrial port as well as a modern yachting marina. What is more, it has been the main port on Turkey's south coast for the last 200 years. During the Crusades, the Christian armies sailed for the Holy Land from here to avoid the long and difficult march across Anatolia. There is a small shingly beach in front of the restored old quarter, but the best beaches are at Lara, 12km east, where many hotels are concentrated.

Karaalı Park

On the clifftops on the road to Lara, this park offers spectacular views towards the mountains of Lycia. It also has a little zoo and some good cliff-edge restaurants.

Museum

Here statues, sarcophagi and mosaics from the ancient cities of the coastal

plain, notably Perge, are on display. Located on the western outskirts of town, on the main road to Kemer. *Open: Tuesday to Sunday, 8am–noon and 1.30pm–5pm. Closed: Monday. Admission free.*

Old port and marina

This is the prettiest part of Antalya, with elaborately carved Ottoman houses clustered on the steep winding lanes above the old port which has now been converted to a swish marina.

Yivli Minare (The fluted minaret)

Antalya's most prominent monument built of the distinctive Seljuk red brick in the 13th century.

ANTALYA ENVIRONS

Aspendos

Here is the finest example of a Roman theatre, indeed of any ancient theatre, anywhere in the world. Aspendos cannot fail to impress. Built in the 2nd century AD, the perfect structure serves today as a venue for wrestling matches and theatrical performances (See **Festivals**, pages 158–9). A track also leads off to the fine Roman aqueduct 1km north of the theatre.

49km east of Antalya, off the E24 and 36km west of Side. Open: daily, 8.30am–5.30pm. Admission charge.

Düden Şelalesi (Düden Waterfalls)

These are a spectacular sight where the Düden river cascades into the sea.
10km from Antalya on the Lara road.

Kurşunlu Şelalesi (Kurşunlu Waterfalls)

Impressive waterfalls 18km north of Antalya on the Isparta road.

Perge

Here stand the extensive ruins of a Hellenistic/Roman city on the flat plain of Pamphylia. Having no defences, it submitted immediately to Alexander the Great on his way through to Persia. Perge has been heavily excavated since 1946, and the major monuments are the theatre with some fine carved reliefs, the stadium, the best preserved in Turkey after that of Aphrodisias, and the circular Hellenistic gate towers built from golden stone, that lead into the main colonnaded street where chariot ruts can still be seen in the paving.
18km east of Antalya, 2km north of the main E24 coast road. Open: daily, 8.30am–5.30pm. Admission charge.

Termessos

A visit to Termessos, known as the Eagle's Nest, is one of the most exciting excursions in Turkey. It takes a good half day to explore, great fun even if ruins do not inspire you. Built in the 4th century BC by a people of legendary fierceness and independence, it is a city set high on pine-clad mountains, now a designated national park.

Exploring the site involves a lot of climbing and walking, so comfortable footwear is important. A network of paths leads all over, and signposts help point the way. Particular highlights not to be missed are the gymnasium, the theatre (whose setting is even more magnificent than that at Pergamum), and the necropolis, or cemetery.
34km northwest of Antalya, off the road to Korkuteli. Reachable only by car or taxi. Open: daily, 8.30am–sunset. Admission charge.

Seljuk bridge *en route* to Aspendos

FETHIYE

Fethiye lies on the western edge of the wild region known as Lycia. In 1981 the tarmac road stopped here and went no further east. The mountainous hinterland was impassable except to donkeys and four-wheel drive vehicles. Now all this has changed, and a new road links all the small towns round the coastline to Antalya, and Lycia is fast becoming one of Turkey's most popular areas with visitors because of its magnificent mountain scenery and beaches, its stunning ancient remains, and its closeness to both Dalaman and Antalya airports.

Set in a wide open bay backed with mountains, Fethiye is a bustling small town, Lycia's main port and fishing centre. Its wide promenade is lined with café bars as it rounds the colourful harbour and small yacht marina. The cobbled streets inland are busy with shops and restaurants, and the daily open-air market is always crowded. There are several discos and nightlife is lively. The town itself has no beach, but Çalış bay is a long sand and pebble beach 4km away reached by a short taxi ride.

Fethiye boasts ancient remains in the group of rock-cut temple tombs in the cliff face above the town, reached by climbing lots of steps. On the summit itself is a crumbling Crusader fortress. In front of the town hall is an enormous sarcophagus, one of Lycia's finest, left here by the earthquakes of 1956 and 1957.

FETHIYE ENVIRONS

Kaya

This is a unique Greek ghost town abandoned in 1923 when the exchange of Greek and Turkish minorities took place and all the 3,500 Greeks returned to Greece. Covering three hillsides, it is an eerie experience to walk round the decaying houses.
5km from Fethiye, off the Ölü Deniz road.

Ölü Deniz, see page 92.

Tlos

This is the site of an ancient Lycian city in a splendid setting high on a rocky promontory above the Xanthos (Eşen) valley. Heavily overgrown and never excavated, Tlos is a charming place to explore, with an acropolis fort, a theatre, baths with seven arched windows, and unusual cliff tombs. The mountains east of the Xanthos valley, called Ak Dağlar, are excellent hiking country (see pages 144–5).
15km from Kemer, which is 22km east of Fethiye, the track is signposted just after crossing the bridge in Kemer. Open: always. Admission free.

FINIKE

Centre of the local tomato and orange production, Finike is a busy agricultural town rather than a resort. It has a working harbour and is set on the western edge of a flat fertile coastal plain. Its hinterland, however, holds several interesting excursions.
118km southwest of Antalya, 182km southeast of Fethiye.

FINIKE ENVIRONS

Arif (Arykanda)

This is a lovely Lycian ruined city set high in the mountains, in the lee of a cliff face overlooking a beautiful green valley with pine forests. Explore the temple tombs, the baths, gymnasium,

theatre and stadium, which sits at the highest point up under the cliff.
35km north of Finike on the Elmalı road. Open: daily, 8.30am–5.30pm. Admission charge.

Kale (Myra)

Formerly known as Demre, this dusty town lies on a flat alluvial plain where tomatoes grow in profusion under plastic sheeting. Set into the hilly outcrop at the back of the town is the surprising ancient city of Myra, with its superbly preserved Roman theatre. Cut into the cliffs behind the theatre is a whole network of rock-cut tombs, some of which bear impressive reliefs of figures celebrating their funeral banquets.

A separate extensive necropolis of rock-cut tombs lies 2km to the east on a track, which includes the so-called Painted Tomb, one of the most remarkable in all Lycia (open: daily, 8.30am–5.30pm; admission charge).

Another surprise in store back in the centre of town is the church of St Nicholas set down in a sunken hollow (open: daily, 9am–4.30pm; admission charge). Nicholas, born in Patara a few kilometres away, was Bishop of Myra in the 3rd century AD. Endowed with miraculous powers for answering the prayers of his supplicants, his cult has come down to us today in the form of Santa Claus (St Nicholas), answerer of children's prayers.

Take time also to visit the beach where the river flows out into the sea, now called Çayağzı, formerly Myra's ancient port of Andriake. (See pages 96–7 for boat trip to Kekova.) On the sandy beach is a cluster of fish restaurants. The huge stone building on the estuary is the ruined Roman granary.
46km east of Kaş, 27km west of Finike.

The Lycian rock tombs at Myra

Limyra

Famous for Lycia's most extensive necropolis, the ancient site of Limyra boasts a theatre, a Byzantine nunnery, and the remarkable tomb of Pericles, a local dynast, set high on a rocky platform overlooking the plain.
8km north of Finike off the Elmalı road. Open: always. Admission free.

LYCIAN TOMBS

Lycia's chief legacy is its tombs. They have survived earthquakes, the ravages of battle and pillaging, and are remarkable today for their sheer profusion, their size and their often dramatic settings cut into cliff faces, littered over hillsides or even submerged in the sea. Many pre-date Alexander the Great.

NOMADS

The Turks regard themselves as a people of nomadic origins descended from the Tu-Kin tribes in the steppes of Mongolia, and it is from this Chinese name that the modern name Turk has evolved. These nomads, fierce fighters and horsemen, swept into eastern Anatolia in AD1067, and the next two centuries saw the flowering of Turkish civilisation under their rule, as they settled and learnt to administer an empire. They never forgot their nomadic roots, and much of their architecture, notably the cylindrical *türbe* (tomb), recalls the pointed tents that used to be their homes.

The Seljuks encouraged the settlement of exceptionally large concentrations of nomads in areas even as far west as Lycia, and until very recently the majority of the population was still semi-nomadic in towns like Kas and Kalkan, migrating with their animals between their suumer pastures (*yaylas*) in the mountains, down to the coastal towns in the winter. A few black goat-hair tents and camels can still sometimes be seen around the Xanthos valley.

A nomad encampment near Urfa

Most nomads in Turkey today however live much further east and have flocks of sheep and goats. They are known as the Yürük, meaning wanderers, and their black tents can be seen in many parts of eastern Anatolia, notably at the foothills around Mount Ararat, and in the Zab valley of Hakkari. The women and children are generally dressed in bright colours and are cheerful, forthright and unveiled, creative in their carpet making.

The traveller Freya Stark wrote of the nomad's lifestyle: *'He does not spend his life as we do altering the accidents that happen to us so as to make them more bearable – but he accepts them with gaiety and endures them with fortitude, and this is his triumph and his charm'.*

KALKAN

A traditional fishing village with a growing number of small hotels and pensions, Kalkan is also a frequent stop for flotillas and yachts. The beaches are manmade. There is a small rocky one in the harbour, but the rest are a short boat ride away, complete with pool and sunbathing terrace. The steep slopes on which the village itself is built run right down to the rocky harbour. Boats also run to nearby bays for secluded swimming. Many of the pensions have idyllic roof terraces where breakfast is served in the mornings, and then they turn into lively bars in the evenings. With its attractive setting, cobbled winding lanes and slightly upmarket feel, Kalkan makes a good base for explorations inland.

25km west of Kaş, 22km southwest of Xanthos.

KALKAN ENVIRONS

Kınık (Xanthos)

Always the greatest city of ancient Lycia, Xanthos is a magnificent site on a hilltop overlooking the Eşen Çayı (Xanthos river). Renowned for their courage, the Xanthians were twice slaughtered in defence of their city.

Seventy crates full of sculptures and inscriptions from the city were shipped off to the British Museum by the first British archaeologists in 1842. The extraordinary pillar tombs beside the theatre date to the 5th and 4th centuries BC. The excavated ruins are extensive and a visit involves quite a lot of scrambling about on small goat paths. Behind the theatre you will find the acropolis with the king's palace and a rock-cut pool. Further afield can be found a Byzantine basilica with mosaic floor, and a cluster of rock-cut tombs near the necropolis.

45km northwest of Kaş, 64km southeast of Fethiye. Open: daily, 8.30am–5pm. Admission charge.

Leton (Letoon)

This pretty site is the sanctuary of Leto, mother of Artemis and Apollo, where ancient festivals of Lycia used to be held. Much of the sanctuary lies underwater today, alive with frogs and tortoises, giving it a special charm. The French excavated here in the 1960s, hence the numbering on the blocks.

4km off the main Fethiye-Kaş road, 4km south of Eşen and 26km from Kalkan. Open: daily, 8.30am–5.30pm. Admission charge.

Patara

Patara boasts a superb sandy beach 22km long and has recently grown a few hotels. It is only a tiny village today but in antiquity, before it sanded up, it was Lycia's port, where the Xanthos river meets the sea. The ancient city has never been excavated, and it is charming now to discover the theatre half-submerged in sand, and the occasional overgrown temple. The most imposing building of all is also the most difficult to reach, the vast long granary of Hadrian, where local grain was stored before being shipped back to Rome.

7km south of Xanthos. The beach is 1km beyond the site. Open: daily, 8.30am–5.30pm. Admission charge.

KAŞ

This is Lycia's most popular resort with many small hotels and quite a chic harbourfront lined with cafés and restaurants. Set in a lovely bay enclosed by high mountains all around, the Greek island of Meis Adası (Kastellorizo) lies directly opposite. The harbour at Kaş is

The Byzantine Basilica at Xanthos

ustling, a frequent destination of many
rivate charter yachts and Turkish *gülets*.
also offers its own daily boat trips to
earby attractions. The main bay does
ot have a swimming beach, but there
re small rocky swimming areas to both
des of the bay where the town has
pread, many of which have been laid
aim to by adjacent hotels or campsites.
hey are not suitable for young children.
ocal fishermen run an efficient and
heap water-taxi service to take you off to
ny favoured bay, returning to collect
ou later.

Modern Kaş occupies the site of
ncient Antiphellus and the remains of
hat Lycian city today can be seen in the
mall theatre above the town and in some
ne sarcophagi scattered about in the
own and harbour. The former Greek
hurch was whitewashed and turned into
mosque in the 1920s.
09km southeast of Fethiye, 73km west of
inike.

KAŞ ENVIRONS
Kekova Adası (Kekova Island), see
pages 96–7.

Meis Adası (Kastellorizo)
Once the finest harbour between Piraeus
and Beirut, this island is all but
abandoned now. Boats run regularly
from Kaş, taking 40 minutes.

THE ORIGINS OF LYCIA
According to Greek legend Leto was
loved by Zeus. Pregnant with her
twins Artemis and Apollo, she was
forced to flee by Hera, jealous wife of
Zeus. Spurned by many cities, she
finally arrived at Letoon and gave
birth. Wolves guided her to the River
Xanthos where she washed her
children and drank. In gratitude she
called the land Lycia for the wolves,
lykos being Greek for wolf.

KEMER

Kemer is a busy and popular family resort which has remained low-rise so the feel is still of a small town rather than a concrete jungle. The beaches are good, both sand and shingle, and kept immaculately clean. There is a bustling marina, and the Moonlight Beach complex (open to the public for a small admission charge) offers excellent sports and watersports. At the Yürük (Nomad) Theme park you can watch traditional craftwork in action. The shops sell carpets and other goods of excellent quality and the place has quite a sophisticated atmosphere. The setting, backed by Lycia's high mountains, is very lovely. Kemer is also well placed for sorties to Lycia's antiquities or to Antalya.

30km south of Antalya.

KEMER ENVIRONS

Faselis (Phaselis)

This is an ancient Lycian city with three natural harbour bays where swimming is a delight. The pine-covered slopes drop right down to the shoreline, giving lots of shade in the tree-covered ruins where you can explore the main paved street, the theatre and baths, the aqueduct just metres from the water's edge. Sarcophagi are scattered about here and there in the undergrowth.

13km south of Kemer, 57km south of Antalya. Open: daily, 8.30am–5.30pm. Admission charge.

Olimpos (Olympos)

Now set within its own national park, this ancient ruined city takes its name from Mount Olympos, and the whole district is heavily wooded and mountainous. A river estuary meets the

sea at Olympos and the valley is overgrown with pink oleander bushes tumbling in profusion everywhere. Olympos has never been excavated, but enthusiasts can find in the undergrowth a theatre, baths, a basilica and temple. The pebble beaches provide excellent swimming. A short drive or long walk from the beach takes you to the mountainside where flames leap out spontaneously. Referred to as *ateş* locally, meaning fire, this was held in antiquity to be the site of the Chimaera, the fire-breathing monster of the underworld.

31km south of Phaselis, 44km south of Kemer. Open: daily, 8.30am–5.30pm. Admission charge.

ÖLÜ DENIZ (DEAD SEA)

This lagoon offers Turkey's most beautiful beach (and busiest), encircled by high pine-clad mountains which plunge straight down into the turquoise sea. It has now been designated a conservation area, so there are only a handful of small hotels and restaurants down on the beach itself (those that were there before the legislation), and the bulk of the accommodation is 4km inland in small villages, but linked by cheap and frequent *dolmuş* taxis. Little boats can be hired from the beach to explore the nearby island of Gemili with its Byzantine churches. Yachts are not allowed to enter the lagoon itself.

17km south of Fethiye. Open: daily, 8am–6pm. Admission charge to the lagoon itself.

SIDE

Side is unique in that the modern resort is actually set among the ruins of the ancient city in between long stretches of sandy beach. It offers a host of hotels, motels, pensions, campsites and restaurants, yet despite all the development, the old town centre, which is largely a pedestrian precinct, has retained its own identity. It has long been a favourite with Turks as well as foreigners, so its atmosphere is that of a genuine, lively Turkish resort, less spoilt than Bodrum, Marmaris or Kuşadası. The old town sits on a small promontory with long sandy beaches on either side. The stroll across the promontory from one beach to the other takes you through the old Roman city, mingled with the town of red tiled roofs and narrow stone-walled alleyways. The shops are particularly colourful and bustling, offering a fine selection for present-buying, especially in jewellery, onyx and carpets.

There is a small fishing harbour, barely noticeable from the beach, and, not having a marina, it is free from yachts and *gülets*.

Of all the ancient cities on Turkey's southern shore, Side is the only one to have been systematically excavated. The city flourished under the Roman Empire, and most of the extant monuments date from that period. The splendid theatre, seating 17,000, is one of the largest in Asia Minor, and the top seats afford splendid views over the agora, museum, baths, temples, and to the beaches beyond.

Less than an hour's drive from Antalya and its airport, Side is also a good base for exploring the region. Cars have to be left in the carpark just beyond the Roman archway.

3km east of Antalya, 66km west of Alanya on the E24 coast road. Site museum open: Tuesday to Sunday, 9.30am–5.30pm. Closed: Monday. Admission charge.

Temple of Apollo at Side. Although Greek in origin, most of the city's ruins are Roman

SIDE ENVIRONS

Manavgat Şelalesi (Manavgat Waterfalls)

A lovely spot for lunch in summer, the waterfalls are more like rushing rapids than true falls. A series of souvenir shops herald the approach, and inside the fenced-off area an extensive restaurant is laid out with some tables scattered under trees, some perched up on individual platforms in the rushing water itself.

7km northeast of Side up a signposted fork off the E24 coast road. Open: daily, 8.30am–6pm. Admission charge.

Selge, see pages 98–9.

Lycia Walk: Cadyanda

This excursion offers the chance to see some of Lycia's magnificent mountain scenery well away from the crowds of the coast, culminating in a climb to Cadyanda, a little-known ancient hilltop city. You can walk along easy forest tracks for an hour or so to reach the summit, and then spend an hour exploring the picturesquely overgrown ruins of Cadyanda. *Allow half a day for the whole outing from Fethiye, but it could easily make a relaxing day trip too.*

To reach Cadyanda, leave Fethiye by the main coast road to Marmaris, then fork off inland after 3km towards Üzümlü, 20km to the north.

ÜZÜMLÜ

At the village the tarmac ends, but a drivable track continues

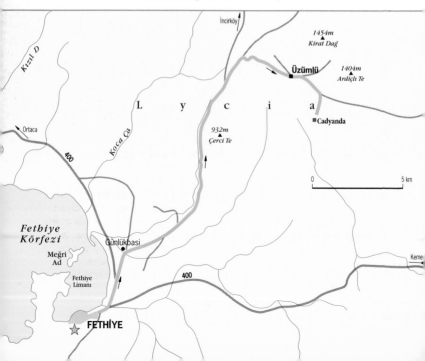

and Cadyanda is marked on a yellow sign pointing straight out beyond the village.

Leaving your car by the domed cistern in the fields 600m beyond the village, the walk up the forest track to reach the ancient city of Cadyanda takes just over an hour. If you want to shorten the walk, drive on to the highest point of the track, where there is a little parking area, and from where it is only half an hour's walk to the top.

DRAMATIC VIEWS

The scenery all around is magnificent – Lycian landscapes in all their majesty. The forested hills drop away to the Xanthos valley and beyond it rise the distant peaks of Ak Dağ, the White Mountain.

THE NECROPOLIS

Take the wide path from the parking area that seems to lead a little downhill at first, and this will lead you after 30 minutes or less to a wide open necropolis area of Roman stone-built tombs, some with carving round their doors.

THE THEATRE

Above the necropolis, through the trees, you will notice a steep earthy slope that ends in the remains of the city walls of Cadyanda, and immediately behind them lies the charmingly rustic theatre, with trees growing up through the seats. The pit dug in the centre of the semi-circle is the work of a hopeful treasure-seeker – in all parts of rural Turkey villagers were convinced that ancient ruins contained treasure. Why else would foreigners spend so long poking around among these old stones?

THE CITY CENTRE

Climbing to the top of the theatre a small

One of the Roman tombs in the Necropolis area

path can be found that leads up through the forest past some vast open cisterns still full of stagnant water, to the centre of the city, where you will find the baths, the largest buildings still standing, and a big stadium, heavily grassed over but with seats intact along one side. The setting, in a grassy clearing in the forest, is tranquil and relaxing; an excellent picnic spot.

Kekova Boat Trip

This outing in a boat makes an enjoyable and relaxing day, combining a swim and a simple lunch out at a village restaurant with a visit to several ancient Lycian cities in and around the island of Kekova about 30km from Kaş. Some of the cities are partly underwater as a result of earthquakes over the centuries.

Tickets for the trip can be bought from Kaş harbour, and the boat leaves at 9am, returning around 6pm. Off season, or if you find that you have missed the large boat, you can negotiate a price with any fisherman in the harbour to take you instead. This is obviously more expensive, but has the advantage that you can dictate the timing.

Boats to visit Kekova can also be hired from Çayağzı, the harbour of Kale (Demre), a little further to the east, actually a lot closer to Kekova than Kaş. Take a mask and flippers for snorkelling round the underwater ruins. *Allow one day.*

The foundations of submerged buildings at Kekova Island

The daily boat ploughing the waves between the mainland and Kekora Island

As the boat leaves Kaş harbour, it first passes the island of Meis Adası (Kastellorizo); then after about 90 minutes, the ruins of Aperlae, a Lycian town dating from the 4th century BC.

APERLAE

The spot is uninhabited now and the nearest village is an hour's walk inland. The town walls are the best preserved remains at Aperlae, and in the shallow water of the bay, your captain will point out whole streets and the outline of buildings now submerged. The spot is rather rocky for a swim and it is better to leave that for the next stop.

TERSANE

A further 45 minutes' cruising brings you to a lovely cove on Kekova island with a Byzantine church apse standing just offshore. This is called Tersane, and is an excellent swimming spot, though watch out for spiky black sea urchins if you swim over to look at the submerged houses at the edge of the bay. Skin-diving is forbidden here.

Back on board, the boat skirts the edge of Kekova island where rock-cut stairways, house foundations, and the occasional door lintel can be made out underwater. Then the boat heads across the narrow straits to the mainland.

SIMENA

The ancient site of Simena stands above the current village of Kale (castle), named after the Byzantine fort with its crenellated walls on the summit. Lunch is generally taken at one of the simple restaurants here in the harbour overlooking more submerged ruins and the occasional Lycian sarcophagus standing in the water.

After lunch it is worth climbing up through the village to the fort to find the charming tiny rock-cut theatre set near the summit. More huge sarcophagi, so typical of Lycia, are scattered about the hillsides.

The boat journey back to Kaş takes about 2½ hours. From Çayağzı it is only about an hour, but fewer boats run as there are less people to fill them.

Selge Canyon Walk

This drive and walk gives the chance for visitors who are based in a coastal resort like Side or Alanya to sample the delights of inland Turkey, with the ruined ancient city of Selge as the final goal. The scenery throughout is magnificent, with gorges and mountains, a striking contrast to the flatness of the coastal plain.

In the heat of summer it can provide a pleasant escape, as the air is noticeably cooler than on the coast and there is a constant breeze. Selge itself lies at an altitude of 1,000m. *The trip should be regarded as a full day's excursion from your base, and after driving to reach the starting point, the amount of walking is up to you, and can be anything from one to six hours.*

Selge is reached by turning off the main E24 coast road between Side and Antalya, at the signpost marked Beşkonak and Köprülükanyon Milliparkı (National Park of the Canyon with the Bridge). The total drive from Side is 90km and takes about 80 minutes, passing through pretty wooded foothills with glimpses of the wide Eurymedon river below. Beyond Beşkonak the narrow road continues for a further 6km to reach the famous Roman bridge over the canyon.

ROMAN BRIDGE

The starting point of the full walk is the Roman bridge, a superb construction across the canyon and river, as sound

An impressive feat of early engineering, the Roman bridge spanning the Eurymedon river

day as the day it was built. Just before
is a charming restaurant on a shady
rrace with extraordinary tables up on
e-house platforms overhanging the
ver, a welcome stop for beer and
babs on your return.

Driving or walking according to time
d preference, follow the sign to
ltınkaya 14km, which forks left after
e restaurant to lead across the bridge,
en forks right.

AIRY CHIMNEYS

he narrow road zigzags steeply to
imb the 700m from the bridge, and as
u near the plateau where the village of
ltınkaya and the ruins of Selge lie, you
ill notice weird rock formations called
iry chimneys, the result of wind
osion. There are fabulous precipitous
ews across the mountains and valleys,
ith no habitation anywhere until the
ltivated fields around the village are
ached. The fairy chimneys are a good
ace to leave the car if you want a much
ore leisurely walk, as it takes about 15
inutes from here to reach Selge.

LTINKAYA AND ANCIENT
ELGE

s you approach, the ancient theatre
ses imposingly behind the village with
backdrop of snow-covered mountains.
he track leads through the village and
imbs up to reach the theatre from
chind, so that you pop straight on to
e top seats with wonderful views. The
ontrast between what must have been a
ourishing city and the poverty of the
illage seen today could hardly be more
triking. The village children are
harming and invariably insist on
ccompanying you on your tour.
ncient capitals and marble blocks now
umbly serve as garden furniture in the

Still waters in the rocky Köprülü Canyon *en
route* to Selge

yards of village houses.

From the top of the theatre a path
leads off to the west along the ridge of
the hill and leads through foundations
and tumbled columns to what seems to
have been the ancient main street with
evidence of the drainage system
underneath. This street leads to the
agora paved in fine flagstones with much
ancient carving scattered about,
including a lovely white marble bull's
head. On the hillock beyond the agora
are the remains of a Christian basilica
from the days when Selge was the seat of
a bishop in Byzantine times.

A scramble down the front of this
hillside gives a view of the ancient city
walls. Rejoin the track beside the old
Roman spring where a small amount of
drinkable water still trickles out.

Ankara and Central Anatolia

*H*ere visitors enter a different Turkey, far removed from the familiar resor
of the coast. These heartlands of Turkey are largely bleak and inhospitable,
central plateau over 1,000m high, denuded of vegetation by geology and cl
mate. Scattered about on this plateau, however, are some strange surprise
sometimes caused by geology – like the volcanic freak of Cappadocia (se
pages 110–15) – sometimes caused by man overcoming the elements, as in th
Hittite capital at Boğazkale (see pages 106–7).

The best way to travel in this region is
by car or bus. The bus network between
main towns here operates as efficiently
as it does elsewhere in Turkey. There is
a railroad that runs from Eskişehir to
Ankara, then continues southeastwards
to Kayseri on the edge of Cappadocia,
and if you do not have a car, this can be
an exciting journey as it follows many
river gorges along the plateau. The

railway between Sivas and Erzincan
takes you to Divriği and then passes
through one of the most dramatic river
gorges in all Turkey.

Ankara straddles the divide in
Turkey between the cosmopolitan,
western regions which are projecting
themselves towards Europe, and the
colossal Asian landmass to the east
where traditional customs and values

ANKARA AND CENTRAL ANATOLIA

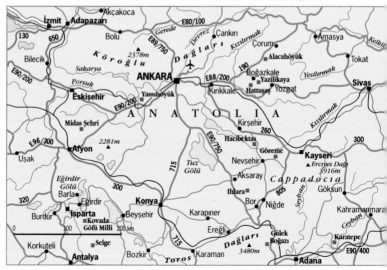

have changed little. The sophisticated westernised Turk with his soft Istanbul accent becomes harder to find, and the rougher side of the Turkish character comes to the fore, the accent growing more guttural.

ANKARA

Ankara is a curious city. As modern Turkey's capital it has many roles to play, and it is the conflict of these roles that makes the city intriguing today. Set in the heart of the Anatolian plateau, Atatürk chose it in a deliberate move away from the Byzantine and Ottoman associations of Istanbul and its past.

Ironically for a city created as a home for a centralised bureaucracy, planning was tossed to the winds just a few years after its rise to capital status, in a speculative rush, and the influx of rural immigrants seeking a better life in the big city.

The entire city is set within a basin on a series of small steep hills. The wide main boulevards run in straight lines along the open valleys, while the narrow sidestreets zigzag uphill among the 'gecekondu' areas (literally 'night lodgings'). These are the houses of the rural immigrants, huddled together covering every inch of ground, painted in blues, greens, mauves and yellows, where the bulk of Ankara's 3 million population lives. When Atatürk moved here in 1919 Ankara was a town of only 30,000. In 1960 it still had only 500,000. In winter the basin setting traps the brown fumes from the lignite which is burnt for heating fuel, but this is expected to improve shortly with the introduction of city gas piping.

Though it is Turkey's new capital, Ankara is far from being a new city. The main streets are lined with luxury high-

Enticing sacks of spices lined up outside a stall in the old quarter of Ankara

rise hotels, European-style restaurants and cafés, impressive new embassies and government buildings, while the old cobbled streets round the citadel seem like a different world with traditionally dressed peasants living much the same as ever.

Given Ankara's background, it is fitting that the two major sights the city has to offer the visitor today should reflect its ancient and its modern ties: the Anadolu Medeniyetleri Müzesi (Museum of Anatolian Civilisations) and Anıt Kabir (Atatürk's Mausoleum). Taxis are cheap and efficient and distances small.

Ankara is located 459km from Istanbul, 250km from Konya, 506km from Antalya and 433km from Samsun. Ankara's airport (Esenboğa) lies 28km to the north of the city, 30 minutes' drive from the centre. A dual-carriageway highway now links Ankara with Istanbul, replacing the previous narrow and overloaded road.

ANIT KABIR (ATATÜRK'S MAUSOLEUM)

Visitors to this tomb can see in tangible form the personality cult built around this remarkable man who died in 1938 but whose picture still hangs in every private house and public place. The sheer scale of the monument is overwhelming: the area occupies an entire hill of beautifully kept gardens

ANKARA

Roma Hamamları

HİPODROM

İSTANBUL CADDESİ

SEBZEBANCELERİ BOKAĞI

Atatürk Kültür Mrk

KAZIM KARABEKİR CADDESİ

HİPODROM CADDESİ

ULUS

İSTİKLÂL CADDESİ

CUMHURİYET

19 Mayıs Stadyum

Ankara Garı

CELAL BAYAR

Gençlik Parkı

Opera

TALAT PAŞA

BAHÇELİEVLER CADDESİ

MALTEPE

ANIT

TURGUT REİS CADDESİ

GENÇLİK CADDESİ

MUSTAFA KEMAL BULVARI

GAZİ

Anıt Kabir

ANITTEPE

Maltepe Camii

MARESAL FEVZİ ÇAKMAK CADDESİ

AKDENİZ CADDESİ

STRAZBURG CADDESİ

NECATİBEY CADDESİ

İSMET İNÖNÜ BULVARI

DİKMEN CADDESİ

CADDESİ

Konser Salonu

Etnoygrafya Müzesi

Abdi İpekçi Parkı

CEMAL GÜRSEL CADDESİ

SIHHİYE

ATATÜRK BULVARI

MITHAT PAŞA CADDESİ

ZİYA GÖKALP

MUDAFAA CADDESİ

Bakanlıklar

KIZILAY

MESRUTİYET CADDESİ

ATATÜRK BULVARI

ESAT

Türkiye Büyük Millet Meclisi

Kocatepe Camii

Kurtulus Parkı

LİBYA CADDESİ

Roma Hamamları

Hacı Bayram Camii

Ogüst Mabedi

Julianus Sütunu

HİZARPARKI

ANAFARTALAR

ATATÜRK BULVARI

Merkez Bankası

CADDESİ

Arkeoloji Müzesi

ALTINDAĞ

BENTDERESİ CADDESİ

Ankara Kalesi

Alaattin Camii

HİSAR

CANKIRI SOKAĞI

ALTINDAĞ

CANKIRI CADDESİ

Aslanhane Camii

ULUCANLAR CADDESİ

SAMANPAZARI

CADDESİ

HASIRCILAR SOKAĞI

Hacettepe Üniversitesi

Hacattepe Parkı

Kurtulus Parkı

GÖKALP

MAHMUT ESAT BOZKURT CAD

HASAN ALİ YÜCEL CADDESİ

KIBRIS CADDESİ

KOCATEPE

TUNALI HİLMİ CADDESİ

BULBULDERESİ SOKAĞI

SEYRAN SOKAĞI

YAPRAK CADDESİ

CADDESİ

0   ½   1 km

ristling with smartly uniformed guards. The colossal limestone building itself is a cross between a classical temple and a modern monument. The stone sarcophagus weighs 40,000 kilos.

nt Caddesi. Open: summer, daily, am–5pm; winter, daily, 9am–4pm. Sound nd Light show in summer at 9pm. dmission free.

ANKARA KALESI (CITADEL)

A 10-minute walk up from the Museum of Anatolian Civilisations brings you to the oldest part of Ankara whose foundations date back to the 3rd century BC. The defence walls visible today are Byzantine and Ottoman, and in the narrow streets within children still play barefoot in the dust oblivious to the pace of change in the modern city below.

ANADOLU MEDENIYETLERI MÜZESI (MUSEUM OF ANATOLIAN CIVILISATIONS)

The idea for starting such a collection was, like every idea in Ankara, Atatürk's. It was originally called the Hittite Museum to draw the world's attention to the newly discovered mountain culture of Anatolia. Small but carefully and clearly laid out, the museum has indeed achieved renown as the most spectacular and comprehensive display of Hittite and Urartian finds in the world. The building itself, set in colourful well-kept gardens full of statues and benches, is a renovated 15th–century Ottoman *bedestan* (covered market), which lends itself well to a museum layout because visitors progress chronologically round all four sides from neolithic to Roman. In the central courtyard, the monumental stone Hittite carvings are displayed.

Do not miss the Anatolian earth mother, grotesquely fat by modern

standards, with bulging arms, legs, breasts and belly. Female fatness was admired until very recently in Turkey. An Ottoman saying ran: 'She is so beautiful she has to go through the door sideways'. *Anafartalar Caddesi. Open: summer, 8.30am–noon and 1.30pm–5.30pm; winter, 8.30am–12.30pm and 1pm–5pm. Closed: Monday. Admission charge.*

ROMAN ANKARA

A handful of Roman monuments remain in Ankara, the principal ones being the Ogüst Mabedi (Temple of Augustus), the Julianus Sütunu (Column of Julian) and the Roma Hamamlari (Roman baths). They are all off Çankırı Caddesı, and admission is free.

Atatürk's Tomb, with soldiers permanently standing guard

THE HITTITES

Until a century ago the Hittites were a mystery race mentioned only in the Old Testament (Uriah the Hittite) and in ancient Egyptian hieroglyphs.

Then in 1834 the first archaeological evidence of their existence was discovered at Boğazkale (Hattusas) in central Anatolia, and later excavations revealed thousands of cuneiform tablets which pieced together the history of the lost Hittite Empire.

The most remarkable thing about the Hittites is that, contemporary with the valley cultures of the ancient Egyptians and Babylonians, they were the only early civilisation to thrive in inhospitable mountain country. They were not indigenous but came in a great surge originally

Hittite gods at the Ankara Museum of Anatolian Civilizations

from southern Russia and central Asia. From their capital Hattusas they ruled Anatolia from the 19th to the 13th century BC. Practical and intellectually unpretentious, they devised a body of 200 laws covering every crime they could imagine.

Murder, black magic and theft could all be compounded by a money payment or by restitution of property. The offences they singled out for capital punishment were defiance of the state, rape and sexual intercourse with animals. For

Hittite Storm God, Ankara Museum

Left: the War God on the King's Gate, Boğazkale. Below: detail from Hittite sculpture

currency they used silver bars or rings.

Their most enduring legacy today is their powerful rock sculpture, simple colossal representations of Hittite gods, especially their weather god Teshub, their sacred bull and lions guarding gateways.

The emergence of the Hittites from almost total obscurity has been one of the great achievements of archaeology this century. As most of the research into this civilisation has been reported by German and Czech scholars, it is not as famous in the English-speaking world as it deserves to be. It was in fact one of the greatest Bronze Age civilisations, speaking one of the earliest recorded of the Indo-European family of languages, the source of all tongues spoken in Europe, India and beyond.

The great arch is now collapsed but the Lion Gate at Boğazkale is still guarded by its creatures

CENTRAL ANATOLIA

AMASYA

Birthplace of the famous geographer Strabo in 64BC, Amasya was the capital of the Pontic Empire, a small freak kingdom founded by a Greek tyrant. Today it is visited for its pretty river setting with timbered Ottoman houses overhanging the bank, and for the Pontic remains on the cliffside. A sign points over the bridge to Kızlar Sarayı (Maidens' Palace) and Kralkaya (King's Rock), the latter involving a steep ascent to the dramatic kings' tombs carved out of the hard basalt. A few attractive Islamic buildings have also survived down in the town.

A ruined lunatic asylum, built in 1308 under the Mongol ruler Tamerlane, stands on Amasya's river front. Fountains and running water were frequently used in the treatment of the mentally ill. The barbaric Mongol hordes overran most of Anatolia, leaving a trail of destruction behind from which it took the Ottomans 50 years to recover.

352km northeast of Ankara, 183km northeast of Boğazkale and 127km south of Samsun. The cliff sites are always open, admission free.

BOĞAZKALE (HATTUŞAŞ)

The Hittite capital of Boğazkale covers a vast area and to explore it on foot would take three or four hours. A car is advisable to reduce the effort of the long steep shadeless climb, especially in summer.

The site is a three-cornered rocky plateau bordered by two valleys and does not lend itself easily to building because of the uneven surfaces, so the planners of 3,000 years ago had to build up artificial terraces. Boğazkale means fortress of the narrow mountain pass, and the site was chosen because of its naturally defensive topography and because of the unusual abundance, in central Anatolian terms, of brooks and springs. The defence wall was 6.5km long, with 200 towers.

The first Hittite king called himself Hattusili, the one from Hattuşaş, and later kings had wonderful names like Suppiliuma and Muwatalli and Shubbiliuma.

Today's remains are not the tall pillars and magnificent theatres familiar from western Turkey. Mostly you will see only foundations and low walls, but what impresses is the size and scale of all the buildings. At each of the three corners of the top plateau stand the three city gates, Lion Gate, Sphinx Gate and the King's Gate, all about 500m apart. Start with Lion Gate and notice the lion's characteristically Hittite carved mane, whiskers and hairy chest. The Sphinx Gate's sphinxes are now in museums but you can walk through the 70m long postern tunnel, a remarkable piece of military engineering. King's Gate bears a copy of the original smiling war god now in the Ankara museum.

Lower down are the fortified royal palaces, and then the great temple of the weather god, the largest and best preserved of any Hittite temple, surrounded by 78 storerooms, some still with colossal storage jars for wine and oil.

206km east of Ankara, 181km southwest of Amasya. Open: daily, 8.30am–6pm. Admission charge.

BOĞAZKALE ENVIRONS

Alacahöyük

This is a much more compact city than Boğazkale, and conveys more clearly the feel of a fortified Hittite town. You can walk along the main street with its Hittite drainage, admire the elaborate reliefs on the Sphinx Gate and discover the ingenious underground postern tunnel. There is a small museum on site.
36km north of Boğazkale. Open: daily, 8.30am–noon and 1.30pm–5.30pm. Admission charge.

Yazılıkaya

This is the extraordinary 13th-century BC rock-cut open-air sanctuary of Hattuşaş, set in a group of rock clefts among pine trees, unique of its kind. Apart from Karatepe (see page 81), it is the only Hittite site to have all its rock reliefs in situ. The main gallery shows 42 warrior gods walking to the right, and 21 goddesses walking to the left. The second gallery has four smaller but better-preserved reliefs.
3km east of Boğazkale. Open: daily, 8.30am–6pm. Admission charge.

Detail from Sphinx Gate, Alacahöyük

KONYA

Konya is Turkey's most religious city, home of the mystic Sufi sect of Islam and its famous Whirling Dervishes. Their centre was the Mevlana Tekke, the heart of Konya, with its unforgettable blue-green dome, which remains the highlight of any visit today.

Besides the Mevlana Tekke, Konya also has a number of beautiful Seljuk buildings dating from the 12th and 13th centuries when Konya served as capital for the Seljuks and was a haven of Muslim art and culture.

Apart from these lovely buildings, Konya itself is not a prepossessing place. A city of the steppe, it is a small oasis of relative greenery ringed by vast bleak horizons. Most exploration is best done on foot, as the major monuments are concentrated within a square kilometre. Konya is also noted as the centre of Turkey's carpet trade, and you will doubtless be lured at least once into a carpet shop.

Konya lies 250km south of Ankara, 256km northwest of Silifke.

Mevlana Tekke

This sacred shrine and object of Muslim pilgrimage from all over Turkey is where Mevlana (see pages 118–9) was buried in 1273. It is now a museum and awed visitors creep respectfully from one exhibit to another, the atmosphere of reverence being almost tangible.

It was round the fountain in the front courtyard that the dervishes whirled. The heavily decorated dervish tombs lie inside the main building, draped in richly embroidered cloths and with the distinctive turban on top. Mevlana's own is covered in his own poetry, and the blue-green dome rises directly above his tomb. The displayed treasures were all

gifts from sultans and princes to the Mevlevi order.

Kışla Caddesı. Open: daily, 9am–noon and 1.30pm–5.30pm. Admission charge.

Alaeddin Mosque

The largest mosque in Konya, it took 70 years to build. Eight Seljuk sultans are buried inside. It is set at the foot of the Alaeddin Park, the former acropolis in Roman times, where there are gardens and cafés. Completed in 1221, it is still a working mosque.

Alaeddin Bulvarı.

Karatay Medrese

Opposite the Alaeddin mosque stands this theological college built in 1258, with a magnificently carved entrance portal. It is now a museum for Seljuk and Ottoman tiles. The interior domed ceiling is stunningly decorated with yellow stars against a deep blue background.

Alaeddin Bulvarı. Open: daily, 9am–noon and 1.30pm–5.30pm. Admission charge.

KONYA ENVIRONS

Alahan Monastery

This remote ruined Byzantine monastery complex in its magnificent mountain setting should not be missed. Built at the end of the 5th century, approaching visitors first see the great western basilica with elaborate relief sculptures of the archangels Gabriel and Michael trampling pagan gods underfoot. The eastern church was built about 50 years later, and is beautifully preserved, with an appearance of grace and elegance.

161km southeast of Konya, 24km northwest of Mut. Open: daily, 8.30am–sunset. Admission charge.

Mevlana Monastery, Konya, is built around the mausoleum of the dervishes order's founder, Rumi

SIVAS

One of the Seljuk Empire's principal cities, Sivas is still adorned with beautiful Seljuk buildings. The most famous is the Çifte Minare Medrese (Twin Minaret Madrasa), prominent in the main square. Curiously, it is only a façade, the main structure having collapsed long ago. The other major monuments are the Gök Medrese, the Şihafiye and Buruciye Medrese, and the Ulu Camii with its leaning tower. *441km east of Ankara, 220km southeast of Amasya.*

SIVAS ENVIRONS

Divriği

Difficult to reach by road, Divriği is one of the few places it may be best to get to by train, as the Sivas–Erzincan line runs through it. The reason for visiting at all is the extraordinary 13th-century mosque-madrasa complex, a unique architectural phenomenon, almost reminiscent of something from the Indian Moghul Empire.

165km east of Sivas, 192km north of Malatya. Open: daily, 8.30am–6pm. Admission free, but tip the guardian.

TOKAT

This central Anatolian town is famous for one monument, the Gök Medrese (Turquoise Madrasa), named after the colour of its tiles. Now a restored and prettily laid-out museum, the madrasa was built in 1275.

103km north of Sivas, 117km east of Amasya. Open: daily, 9am–noon and 1.30pm–5.30pm. Admission charge.

TOKAT ENVIRONS

Sulusaray (Sebastopolis)

This Roman city was only discovered in 1988, after a flood uncovered some of its marble columns. Its state of preservation promises to rival Ephesus, showpiece of the Aegean. Large sections of marble flooring and a gymnasium have been excavated, but it will be many years before the work is completed.

38km southwest of Tokat.

Cappadocia

*T*his unique region of volcanic landscapes and rock-carved churches was largely forgotten by the western world until rediscovered by a French priest, who published his vast research in the 1930s and 1940s. Its renown has now spread worldwide, and Cappadocia has become one of the most visited and photographed areas of Turkey.

The tourist season runs from April to November, but the place always looks lovely in the winter months when there is usually a coating of snow on the fairy chimneys. These chimneys were formed by the effects of wind, snow and rain erosion over the course of millenia, on the soft porous volcanic rock called tufa. Unlike the harsh greys and blacks associated with most volcanic rock, the tufa has shades of yellow, pale grey, mauve, pink and umber, reflecting its mineral richness. The softness of the tufa lent itself to easy tunnelling, and various accidents of history meant that early Christians sought refuge from persecution here in cities they carved out underground. Over the 7th to the 14th centuries, monasticism flourished here, and hundreds of tiny churches were carved out of the rock, many of them containing fine paintings which have provided us with a remarkable record of religious art.

Despite the tourist invasion, it is still possible to escape the madding crowd in the lesser known valleys like Soğanli and Ihlara. The best range of accommodation is to be found in Ürgüp, Avanos and Nevşehir. The sheer number and variety of places to visit can be bewildering on a first visit. Here are some suggested day itineraries to help plan your stay.

1 Göreme Valley, Üçhisar (lunch), Ortahisar, Çavuşin, Zelve.
2 Soğanlı (lunch), Derinkuyu, Kaymakı.
3 Ihlara (lunch), Avanos, Özkonak, Peribacaları Valley.

CAPPADOCIA

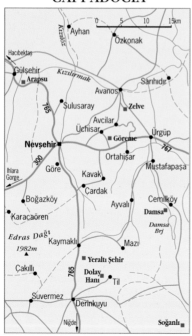

AVANOS

Avanos is a pretty little town on the banks of the Kızılırmak (Red River), Anatolia's longest. The distinctive deep red soil which colours the river water is

The obelisk-like rock chimneys in the
Göreme Valley

much in evidence, and on a rainy day
you and your shoes will soon be covered
in it. The red clay is still used for the
famous pottery, exported from earliest
times to Greece and Rome.

On the road south from Avanos to
Ürgüp, is the famous Peribacaları Valley
of fairy chimneys with a forest of pinkish
cones.

13km northwest of Ürgüp.

ÇAVUŞIN

Noted for two churches, one on the
main road reached by iron steps, and the
other in the village itself. Both have fine
frescos.

*24km northwest of Ürgüp, 7km south of
Avanos.*

DERINKUYU

This amazing underground city was
rediscovered in 1963. The full number
of storeys is thought to be as many as 18
or 20, but only the top eight are open to
the public. Some 20,000 people used to

Derinkuyu, underground city

live here, and the advantages of this
underground lifestyle, apart from the
obvious safety, were constant
temperatures, year-round humidity and
no insects. Ventilation was good by
means of air chimneys. The first two
storeys contained communal kitchens,
storage, stables, toilets, dining halls and
bedrooms, while the lower levels were
hiding places with wells, churches,
armouries, dungeons and graves.
*53km southwest of Ürgüp, 30km south of
Nevşehir. Open: daily, 8am–6pm.
Admission charge.*

Göreme Valley

*T*his open-air museum has now been designated a national park and i
Cappadocia's major tourist attraction. There is no doubt that the churche
within the valley contain the most spectacular paintings of the region, bu
there is a definite sense of being 'processed' through the site along roped-o
walkways, following the arrows, which does detract to some extent from the
enjoyment of the visit.

Göreme was one of the great centres of
Christianity from the 6th to the 10th
century and the Byzantine art on view
here reflects a primitive provincial style,
rich in colour and with an emotional
intensity that was lacking in the
formalism of contemporary work at
Constantinople.

The paintings have been much
damaged over the centuries by graffiti,
mainly of the Byzantine Greeks
themselves. They held that a brew of
water and broken fresco fragments had
miraculous healing powers, and the
supplicant would carve his name and
date beside the chunk he had chiselled
out, to make sure God had registered
who he was.

Most of the later defacement,
literally, of Christ, Mary and the saints
was carried out by local Muslim villagers
for whom representation of the human
form was a heresy, as only God could
create this. Without faces, the figures
were considered dead.
*Göreme Valley is 11km southwest of Ürgüp.
Open: daily, 8.30am–5pm. Admission
charge and car park fee.*

Elmalı Kilise (Apple Church)
An unusual 11th-century church,
entered through a narrow tunnel, and
with a dome over four pillars. There are
fine frescos of the Last Supper, the
Betrayal by Judas and the Crucifixion.

Çarıklı Kilise (Church with the Shoes)
Reached by an iron staircase, the name
comes from the shoeprints at the bottom
of one of the pictures of Christ.

Karanlık Kilise (Dark Church)
Part of a monastery complex whose
façade has now fallen away, exposing the
once dark interior, this church has
colourful 11th-century frescos of the
Three Kings, the Last Supper and the
Betrayal.

SYMBOLISM

The symbolic painting of the
Iconoclastic period when use of the
human form was forbidden, meant that
many symbols with secret meanings
began to be used. Look out for the
following:

pigeon/dove	fertility, peace, love and innocence.
cock	a white one is good luck, a black one is the devil.
peacock	the resurrection of the body.
lion	victory and salvation.
rabbit	sexuality, the devil, magic.
vine	symbol of Jesus.
palm	heaven and eternal life.
fish	the pious followers.

ızlar Kilise (Convent)

his is a large complex on three levels ith a refectory and kitchen, and housed)0 nuns at its height.

okalı Kilise (Church with a Buckle)

oveliest of the churches by far, the okalı lies outside the main ticketed ea. Ask the guardian to open it for »u, as it is by far the biggest of the öreme churches with magnificent escos, set on an exquisite deep blue ıckground. The colours and condition the interior are still superb.

escos in the Çarıklı Kilise, Göreme Valley

St Barbara Kilise (St Barbara Church)

This has the plain red geometric lines of the Iconoclastic period (AD726–843), when all representations of people in religious art were banned in the East. The red paint was made from the local clay.

Yılanlı Kilise (Snake Church)

One of Göreme's most interesting churches, it has an arched ceiling and is famous for the remarkable painting of St George and the dragon, represented here as a snake, with the damned wrapped in its coils.

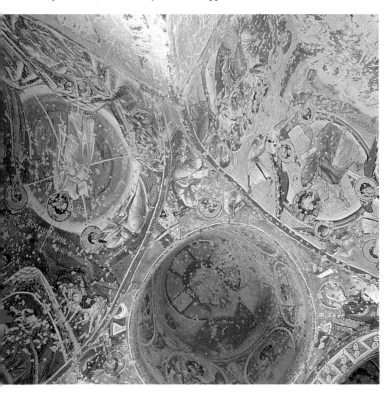

HACIBEKTAŞ

Haci Bektaş was the founder of the Bektaşi Order in the 14th century, and Hacıbektaş is the name of the pretty monastery he established. It is now a museum, visited by many Turks as a holy shrine, and gives visitors an interesting opportunity of seeing how a monastic community lived at that time. The Bektaşi dervishes, or holy men, were much concerned with the rural poor.

68km northwest of Ürgüp, 45km north of Nevşehir. Open: daily, 8.30am–5.30pm. Admission charge

IHLARA GORGE, see pages 116–17.

KAYMAKLI

Smaller than Derinkuyu, this underground city is known to be linked to it by a 9km long tunnel wide enough for four people to walk abreast. Discovered in 1964, it has a mere four storeys.

47km southwest of Ürgüp, 24km south of Nevşehir. Open: daily, 8am–noon and 1pm–6pm. Admission charge.

KAYSERI

The extinct volcano that created the Cappadocian landscapes, Erciyes Dağı (3,916m), rises behind this town. It is notorious for its merchants, especially carpet sellers, whose shrewdness is the subject of several Turkish proverbs. The Seljuk citadel, built of black basalt, is considered one of the finest extant examples of Seljuk military architecture. It has now been turned into a shopping precinct, as befits the local entrepreneurial spirit. Incongruously scattered about the town are several conical *kümbets* (tombs), dating from the 13th and 14th centuries.

328km southeast of Ankara, 87km east of Ürgüp.

ORTAHISAR

Visited for its huge honeycombed fortress which gives fine photographic opportunities over the Cappadocian landscape.

7km southwest of Ürgüp.

ÖZKONAK

The largest of the Cappadocian underground cities, once housing 60,000 people, Özkonak was also the most recently discovered.

25km north of Ürgüp. Open: daily, 8.30am–6pm. Admission charge.

NEVŞEHIR

The largest town of Cappadocia, it offers the visitor nothing beyond a good hotel base. To the north on the Gülşehir road is Açıksaray (Open Palace), where there is an interesting church with an elaborate façade.

23km west of Ürgüp.

NIGDE

A town built round an 11th-century citadel, Nigde boasts a few Seljuk and Mongol monuments of its own, but is visited chiefly for the monastery of Eski Gümüş, 14km to the north off the Kayseri road. This is a very pretty monastery, unique in Cappadocia, with an open courtyard and rooms cut into the rock all around. The main church has delightful frescos.

105km south of Ürgüp. Monastery open: daily, 9am–noon and 1pm–5pm. Admission charge.

SOĞANLI

Taking its name from the pretty troglodyte village that sits above it, the

oğanlı valley divides into two forks,
with signs indicating the location of the
various churches. Of the 60 or so
churches, the most interesting are
Yılanlı Kilise (Snake Church), Saklı
Kilise (Hidden Church), and the
unusual three-storeyed Kubbeli Kilise
(Domed Church) in its own weird rock
formation. They are all in the right-hand
valley fork.
*7km south of Ürgüp. Open: always.
Admission free.*

SULTANHANI

This is the most colossal and best
preserved *caravanserai* in Turkey. Built
in 1232 by the Seljuk sultan Keykubad
I, the *han* provided the travelling
merchant with somewhere to rest and
feed his animals, repair his vehicles, rest
and recuperate himself and be fed, all
free of charge for up to three nights.
Trade under the Seljuks flourished
under such conditions.
*8km west of Aksaray, 108km northeast of
Konya.*

UÇHISAR

Boasting a tall conical cone like
Ortahisar, you can follow the signs to
'Kale' to climb to the top for the views.
At night the cone is illuminated, looking
like some Halloween gourd.
6km west of Ürgüp.

ÜRGÜP

An attractive hilly rural town with
cobbled streets in the heart of the main
Cappadocian valleys, Ürgüp is the best
base for excursions. It still has some old
troglodyte houses of its own, in use as
garages, storerooms or stables.
Cappadocia's museum is here, and there
is good souvenir shopping along the
main street.

The semi-troglodyte town of Ürgüp, the base
from which to explore the Cappadocian valleys

*304km southeast of Ankara, 87km west of
Kayseri and 20km east of Nevşehir.
Museum open: Tuesday to Friday and
Sunday, 8am–5pm. Admission charge.
Located on the main street, Kayseri
Caddesi.*

ZELVE

A pretty series of three valleys dug out
with cave dwellings, making an
attractive walk round various unusual
buildings set in typical Cappadocian
landscapes. The first valley contains a
rock-cut mosque, the only one of its
kind, with a spectacular monastery
complex cut out of a cliff face, requiring
considerable agility to clamber up. A
tunnel links the first valley to the
second, and can be walked through by
torchlight. Churches and a rock-cut mill
can be found in the second and third
valleys.
*19km northwest of Ürgüp, 6km south of
Avanos. Open: daily, 8.30am–6pm.
Admission charge.*

Ihlara Gorge Walk

Lying slightly off the beaten track, this is an excellent trip to escape the crowds at Cappadocia and to explore a few early rock-cut churches set in magnificent gorge scenery. You need to be feeling fairly energetic, as it involves a steep descent into the Ihlara Gorge (formerly called the Peristrema valley by the Greeks), taking about 10 minutes, with the ascent at the end taking about double. *Allow a full half day, or an entire day if you want to do some extra walking.*

To reach Ihlara from Nevşehir involves a scenic drive of 90 minutes southwest. After forking off the main Aksaray road at the yellow sign to Ihlara, the final 30km is along a narrow road dominated by the snow-covered volcano Hasan Dağı, 3,268m high. You pass through a few semi-troglodyte villages, the last of which is Selime at the

entrance to the gorge, where a conical tomb stands on the river bank.

The starting point of the walk lies just before Ihlara village, where you fork left and suddenly come upon a modern resthouse with superb terraces overlooking the gorge. It is open mid-May to mid-November, and offers good food and a handful of rooms for dedicated church explorers.

THE IHLARA GORGE

From the resthouse you embark on the descent into the gorge down the specially built wide concrete steps. There is a ticket office at the top where an admission charge must be paid (open: 8am–sunset).

The 150m deep gorge was formed thousands of years ago by the erosion of the Melendiz river flowing north into Tuz Gölü (the Great Salt Lake). The river itself is the product of melting snow from Hasan Dağı.

Fresco in the Church with a Snake

The Ihlara Gorge, famous for its 6th-century Armenian refugee churches

THE CHURCHES

The major churches in the gorge are signposted, and just before the bottom you come to the first church Ağaçlı Kilise (Church under a Tree). Carved out of the cliff face, it still has well-preserved frescos, most notably of Daniel in the Lion's Den.

Turn right at the valley bottom to reach the Purenliseki Kilise (Church with a Terrace) which has fragmentary frescos. Continuing on the path round a jutting-out cliff where a colossal landslip has occurred, you come to the Kokar Kilise (Fragrant Church) with some attractive paintings outside.

Now retrace your path past the concrete steps to reach the Sümbüllü Kilise (Hyacinth Church), with arches and an elaborate façade carved into the rock. A few metres further on there is a wooden bridge which is crossed to reach the Yilanli Kilise (Church with a Snake),

where the sinners at the Last Judgement are portrayed wrapped in the coils of snakes.

Cross back over the bridge now to reach the other three main churches in the gorge, the Kırk Damlı Kilise (Church with Forty Roofs), the tiny Bahattın Samanlığı (Church with a Granary), and the Direkli Kilise (Columned Church) with three aisles and good paintings.

In the full 16km of the two sides of the gorge, there are over 100 rock-cut churches and several monasteries, and it is very pleasant to wander further afield in search of these if you have the time and energy. The only sounds accompanying the explorer are the rushing river and the wind catching in the poplar trees, and the green fertile river banks are alive with an abundance of small creatures, birds, frogs, lizards and butterflies.

THE WHIRLING DERVISH

Banned in 1925 as part of Atatürk's reform programme to secularise Turkey, the Whirling Dervishes were based in Konya, capital of the old Seljuk empire. The foundation of the Mevlana Order of Whirling Dervishes was the Seljuks' most important contribution to religion.

Celaleddin Rumi, known as Mevlana, is buried in Konya, and every year the internationally famous Mevlana Festival is held here from 9 to 17 December to commemorate his death in 1273. This is the only time when the dervishes can be seen whirling today.

A mystic poet and philosopher, Mevlana believed in ecstatic universal love, a state which he induced by whirling round and round, accompanied by mystical music played on the *ney*, a reed flute. The dance symbolised the revolution of the spheres, and the right hand was held up to receive a blessing from above and the left hand held down to dispense the blessing to the earth below. The dervishes dressed in long white gowns and wore tall felt cones on their heads, as they still do at the annual festival.

Above and below: Dervishes in full flow
Right: Mevlana's tomb under the dome of the Mevlana Tekke, Konya

Eastern Turkey and the Black Sea Coast

*E*astern Turkey remains for most people an unknown, and many are convinced it is largely out of bounds to travellers. Twenty five years ago this was true, but now visitors can travel freely everywhere with the proviso that in the extreme southeast Hakkâri region, you would be advised to stick to the main roads because of Kurdish guerilla activity in the mountains. The Armenian ghost city of Ani does, however, require a permit to visit because of its proximity to the former Russian border, but obtaining it is a simple process from the local tourist office.

The east of Turkey remains very different from the rest of the country. Whole stretches are vast tracts of bleak steppeland, and there are extremes of heat and cold. Yet for all this, there is a

A sheltered bay on the Black Sea, Trabzon Province

power in its sheer scale and roughness that is almost demonic. Extinct volcanoes, snow-capped all year round such as Büyükağrı Dağı (Mount Ararat) lend majesty to the bleakest of horizons. The river and gorge scenery of the Hakkari region, even along the main road, is as beautiful as anything in the

EASTERN TURKEY

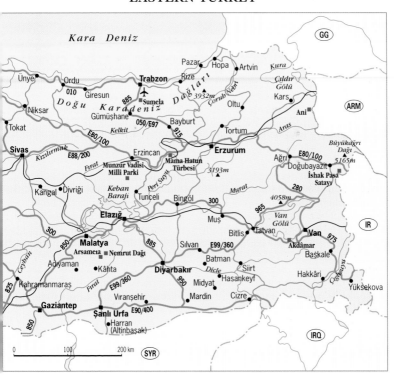

world. Most surreal of all is the vast and eerie Van Gölü (Lake Van).

Moving north towards the Black Sea, there is a sudden contrast from the barren plateau on reaching the wonderfully lush greenness of the Georgian valleys and the Pontic mountains. The whole of the Black Sea coastline is heavily wooded and mountainous, with sand and pebble beaches. It has a few resorts, of which Akçakoca and Amasra are the prettiest, and the inland towns like Safranbolu have impressive traditional timbered houses.

Distances are great in eastern Turkey and many Turks choose to travel by air. There are airports at most large cities, and car hire is available at Adana, Erzurum, Diyarbakır, Malatya and Van airports in eastern Turkey, and at Samsun and Trabzon airports on the Black Sea. Flights, all by Turkish Airlines (THY), connect frequently to Ankara and Istanbul. Private car remains the best way of exploring within the region. Traffic is light, except on the E24 transit route to Iraq and on the E23 to Iran, where heavy lorries can make driving hazardous.

DIYARBAKIR

This great old city backed by the eastern Taurus mountains and sitting on the navigable limit of the Tigris (Dicle) river, dominates the expanse of the northern Mesopotamian plain. Concentrated within its 5km long black basalt walls, the city has the vibrance and vitality that goes with a place that has been important for centuries, and is still a key city of the southeast. Diyarbakır has more historical mosques, churches and other notable buildings than any other Turkish city except Istanbul.

Diyarbakır has a predominantly Kurdish population and has been a natural centre for Kurdish dissident groups, but the tourist today will not notice much tension and can walk freely in all parts of town. That said, walking in the narrow streets within the walls makes keeping your sense of direction difficult. You will inevitably get lost, but distances are too small to make this much of a real problem, and you will soon discover one of the major monuments, all of which have name plaques outside to help you orientate yourself..

In Diyarbakır's monuments, note the distinctive black and white striped effect, achieved by using the pale limestone with the black basalt, both found locally. *Diyarbakır is 188km northeast of Urfa, 548km northeast of Ankara and 402km southwest of Van.*

The Walls and the Citadel

Of the original 72 towers, all but five are still standing. You can walk along the top of them between the Urfa and the Mardin Gates, on a wide grassy path. The Harput Gate is the best preserved and the Saray Kapı (Palace Gate) that leads into the citadel is the most beautiful of the gates.

The Mosques and Churches

Begin with the great 11th-century Ulu Cami, modelled on the Great Umayyad Mosque at Damascus with its decorated archs and columns. The loveliest of the rest are the Safa Mosque, the Iskender Paşa and the Behrem Paşa. You should also visit the Syrian Orthodox church and the Armenian Surp Giragos Church, both of which are still in use, as are all the mosques.

DIYARBAKIR ENVIRONS

Hasankeyf

This spectacularly sited ruined town sits on a cliff overlooking the Tigris. A crumbling 12th-century bridge can still be seen spanning the river, and you can walk up to the 12th-century ruins on the cliff top which cover over 2sq km, complete with palace, mosques, tombs, and private houses.
142km northeast of Mardin, 44km north of Midyat. Open: always. Admission free.

Mardin

Built up on a craggy rock overlooking the Syrian desert, this town is an important Syrian Christian centre with lovely Arab-influenced architecture, all concentrated in the citadel area. The Sultan Isa Medrese built in 1385 is the best example, and there are fine views over the town from its roof. Mardin is sometimes called the 'White City', because of the pale stone used in the buildings, in contrast to black Diyarbakır.

Arnold Toynbee called Mardin the most beautiful town in the world, with some justification. A path leads up from the madrasa to the citadel.
96km southeast of Diyarbakır, 83km northwest of Nusaybin.

Hasankeyf was founded by the Romans as a frontier outpost

Tûr Abdin Monasteries

In this fascinating pocket of land between Mardin, Midyat and Nusaybin, the Syrian Orthodox community flourished from the 5th century onwards. In medieval times there were four bishoprics and 80 monasteries here. Of these four are still functioning with a handful of monks, and the remainder are ruined shells in use as cowsheds or grainstores. Deyrulzaferan (House of Saffron) is the most accessible

monastery, 7km south of Mardin, with one monk and one nun remaining. Visitors can attend evening service at 6pm in Aramaic, the language of Christ.

Midyat is a curious town in two halves, the Christian half with its churches and bell towers, and the Muslim half 2km away. The most flourishing of the monasteries lies 20km east of Midyat, called Mar Gabriel, with six monks, 10 nuns and a bishop. A monk will take you on a guided tour.

DOĞUBEYAZIT

This is a drab frontier town used as the base for the five-day ascent of Büyükağrı Dağı (Mount Ararat, see pages 144–5). The town itself has very little to offer the visitor, but people flock here to see the famous and much photographed Ishak Pasha Saray, the Turkish Taj Mahal, which stands aloft on a hillside 6km away to the south.

Ishak Pasha Saray

This remarkable pleasure palace was built around 1800 on the orders of Ishak Pasha, the local feudal chieftain 'who expressed the wish to have the most beautiful residence in the world, and, after conversing with numerous architects, accepted the services of an Armenian' (Frederick Burnaby, *On Horseback across Asia Minor*). The result is an extraordinary mixture of Seljuk, Persian, Georgian, Armenian and baroque Ottoman styles with stained-glass windows and every possible comfort. To ensure that the Armenian could not design a similar palace for a rival chieftain, his hands were ordered to be chopped off.

Much of the damage and blackening of the walls was caused by the Russian army in the Crimean War, when 400 soldiers slept in the harem rooms intended for Ishak Paşha's 14 concubines.

99km east of Ağri, 228km southeast of Kars and 328km north of Van. Open: daily, 8am–4pm. Admission charge.

ELAZIĞ

A little known place, Elazığ has a remarkable new museum on the campus of the Euphrates University just outside the town. It houses the items salvaged from archaeological digs before the creation of the Keban dam on the Euphrates resulted in the flooding of 50 early settlements. The collection of Urartian (see pages 132–3) objects on display – gold belts, ivories and jewellery – is even more magnificent than that in the Ankara museum. Five kilometres to the north stands the derelict old fortress city of Harput with a 13th-century castle. The magnificent 14th-century castle of Eski Pertek, 24km to the north, is now inaccessible on a rocky outcrop in the new lake.

104km northeast of Malatya, 179km southeast of Divriği. Museum open: 9am–noon and 1.30pm–5.30pm. Admission charge.

ERZINCAN

Destroyed many times by earthquakes, its very name means 'life crusher'. The important Urartian site of Altıntepe lies 16km to the east, where a wealth of gold and bronze metalwork was discovered in tombs untouched by grave robbers. On the hilltop are a well-preserved temple, a palace and a great hall.

190km west of Erzurum, 248km south of Trabzon.

ERZURUM

Set in a great bowl at nearly 2,000m, Turkey's highest provincial capital, Erzurum is a bleak place ringed by broad, eroded mountains. The landscape is harsh and the dull grey stone of the building accentuates it. Culturally, it is something of a highpoint in eastern Turkey, boasting the main university, with strong archaeology and agriculture faculties. Erzurum has two famous monuments, the Yakutiye Medrese, built in 1310 by the Mongols, with pretty turquoise tiling on the minaret, and the Çifte Minare Medrese

The feast room within the harem of Ishak Pasha Saray, Doğubeyazit

(Twin Minaretted Madrasa), built of brick in the 13th century by the Seljuks. Both monuments are in the centre of the old town near the main square and the Ulu Cami (Great Mosque). Both are kept locked and are visible only from the outside. Near by are some Seljuk conical tombs (*kümbets*), and the old Byzantine citadel with its walls still standing and rusting cannon lying around. Its open interior serves as a football pitch for local youths. The new museum on the modern outskirts displays Urartian metalwork and Ottoman jewellery and costumes.

219km southwest of Kars, 322km southeast of Trabzon. Open: 9am–noon and 1.30pm–5.30pm. Admission charge.

KARS

A scruffy town with a suspect sewerage sytem, Kars is rarely visited for its own limited merits, but as a base from which to visit Ani (see below). Kars means snow in Turkish, and the town can be buried in up to 13m of it in winter. Steam locomotives are still in use here, and the train journey from Erzurum takes some seven hours. It has a new museum with a fine *kilim* collection. Other buildings of interest to the visitor are the Armenian Church of the Apostles built in AD932 from black basalt with curious primitive carvings where the apostles look more like gargoyles, and finally the neo-classical Russian buildings now in use as offices throughout the town.

202km southeast of Artvin, 228km northwest of Doğubeyazıt and 219km northeast of Erzurum. Museum open: Tuesday to Sunday, 9am–noon, 1.30pm–5.30pm; admission charge.

KARS ENVIRONS

Ani

A visit to this eerie Armenian ghost town is an unforgettable experience. The contrast of the green fertile landscape with the scenes of devastation all around is a striking one. In the 10th century the city, grown wealthy from its position on an east-west caravan route, outshone anything in Europe, while only Constantinople, Cairo and Baghdad rivalled it in the east. Known as 'Ani of a hundred gates and a thousand churches', what remains today are the colossal walls and the shells of a few of its most robust churches. Earthquakes and Mongol raids in the 14th century destroyed Ani forever. At its height the population was 200,000, nearly four times the current population of Kars.

Because of its location in the 700m of no man's land between the Armenian and Turkish borders, you need a special permit to visit Ani. It takes half an hour to obtain this permit from the Kars Tourist Office (open: 8.30am–12.30pm and 1.30pm–5.30pm), and visitors need passports and car documentation to fill in the forms. If you want to visit Ani the same day, do not arrive at the Tourist Office later than 2.30pm. Ani can only be reached by road, and the drive takes 40 minutes. Taxis can be arranged if necessary.

Ani lies 44km east of Kars.

Tour of Ani

Photography is now permitted on the site, and visitors are no longer given a soldier as escort. The area inside the

Besieged during the Crimean War and finally taken in 1878, Kars remained in Russian hands until the end of the First World War

walls has been laid out in neat paths with signposts. The atmosphere is very silent, almost haunting, yet not in any way frightening. Away from cars and buses, shops and bustle, it is a tranquil experience.

The Armenian/Georgian border (formerly Russian) is formed by the Arpa Cayı, a river set down in the ravine. The former Russian border posts are green and the Turkish posts grey.

St Gregory's Church

Labelled Resimli Kilise (Church with Pictures), this is the loveliest of Ani's remaining churches, built in 1215 with beautiful murals inside and out, painted on a deep royal blue. They depict scenes from the life of Gregory the Illuminator, Apostle to the Armenians.

Cathedral of Ani

The largest Armenian building still standing here or anywhere in Turkey, this late 10th-century church is superbly proportioned with most of its ceiling intact. Like most Armenian architecture, it has a very high ceiling in relation to its length and width. There are no murals, but the beauty lies in the graceful proportions and delicate blind arches.

Menucer Camii

This unusual mosque built in 1072 stands on the edge of the ravine, and the inside feels more like a palace than a mosque.

Church of Gagik I

This church is unique in Armenian architecture in its circular groundplan. Built in 1001, the roundness made it an inherently weaker structure and it has survived the earthquakes less well.

The grubby river of Kars

The ruined 11th-century fortress at Harran replaced a temple dedicated to the moon god Sin

NEMRUT DAĞI

This is one of eastern Turkey's best-known sites, the weird colossal stone heads set on a remote mountaintop. Historically Nemrut Dağı has almost no significance. It is no more than a vast funeral monument to the ruler of a small local dynasty who suffered delusions of grandeur. But for all that, or maybe because of it, it is astonishing and unlike anything else in the world. The kingdom only extended from Adıyaman to Gaziantep, and was called Commagene, established in the 1st century BC. It lasted less than 200 years. Antiochus I, the king who created this sanctuary, depicts himself here surrounded by and as an equal with the gods and great kings, yet he chose such a remote setting on the summit of the 2,150m Nemrut Dağı that it was not discovered until after World War II. The first rough road was built up to it in the 1960s. Before

that, ascent was by donkey and took two days.

The road up leads past a fine Roman bridge over the river Cendere and then past Arsameia, the Commagene capital, where you can explore a cave and tunnel and the heavily ruined town in a lovely grassy hilltop setting.

The road ends a 10-minute walk from the summit, and the rocky path brings you out on to the eastern terrace with the five colossal figures of Apollo, Fortuna, Zeus, Antiochus and Hercules, their heads toppled by earthquakes. The manmade burial mound rises behind and you then walk round to the western terrace where the same five statues face the sunset rather than the dawn.

The only way to reach Nemrut Dağı is the 52km long road, now tarmacked, up from Kâhta, where most of the hotels are situated. The hotels can arrange minibuses. If you are approaching from

yarbakır, a car ferry makes the
nnection across the new Lake Atatürk
e page 138). It takes about one hour
drive up from Kâhta and it is best to
ne your arrival for after midday so that
orning mists have cleared. Dress
armly as the summit is always chilly.
*5km northeast of Adıyaman, 52km north
Kâhta, 362km northeast of Adana,
17km west of Diyarbakır, 263km
utheast of Malatya.*

EMRUT DAĞI ENVIRONS

arran
short drive from Urfa, Harran is
here the Bible tells us Abraham lived
til he was 75. Visitors come to see the
ud-brick beehive houses, thought to be
rgely unchanged since biblical times
art from the TV aerials. There is also
large, ruinous 11th-century fortress
d great mosque.
*5km south of Şanlı Urfa, 25km north
the Syrian border.*

alatya
sprawling commercial city
oted for its apricots, with quite
ophisticated shopping for eastern
urkey, Malatya also has one or
vo unusually good
estaurants for the east
ee **Food and
rink**, page 175).
ive kilometres to
e north is a neo-
ittite site called
slantepe (Lion
ill), whose lions
ow grace the
nkara museum.
*87km north of
diyaman, 104km
uthwest of Elazığ.*

Şanlı Urfa (Urfa)

Named Edessa by Alexander the Great, this ancient city later became the earliest Christian centre in Mesopotamia. Today it is a sprawling dusty city of no beauty, but is visited for its biblical associations with Abraham and the Halil er-Rahman mosque with its lovely Pool of Abraham. Legend has it that Nimrod, King of Assyria, threw Abraham on a funeral pyre here in anger at Abraham's destruction of the idols in his temple. To save him, God created a lake to put out the fire. Abraham is a revered prophet for Muslims as well as Christians, which is why the pool and mosque have become a place of pilgrimage for Muslims. The pool is alive with sacred carp which it is forbidden to kill, and overcrowding is becoming a problem. The area all around is pleasant for strolling with attractive cafés set in gardens. Beyond the pool, concrete steps lead up to the Crusader citadel where two columns are known as the Throne of Nimrod.
149km east of Gaziantep on the E24, 192km west of Mardin.

King Antiochus himself, Nemrut Dağı. He claimed descent from Alexander the Great and Darius the Great of Persia

Water into wine, Sumela Monastery

SAMSUN

The biggest town and port on Turkey's Black Sea coast, its population is now 300,000, having doubled in the last 10 years as a result of urban migration. The coastline to the west of Samsun is generally not as attractive as the stretch to the east, as it is flatter and more built-up. For Black Sea scenery at its best with the green hillsides of the tea plantations tumbling right down to the sea, you need to follow the coast road from Ordu (168km east of Samsun) eastwards

through Trabzon to Hopa near the Georgian border.
365km west of Trabzon.

SUMELA

This ruined monastery and Nemrut Dağı are probably the two most visited sites in eastern Turkey. Clinging Tibetan-like to a sheer rock face above steep and heavily wooded slopes, it is a stiff 30-minute climb from where the road ends to reach the monastery. Far from any habitation and often shrouded in mountain mists, it has a haunting quality despite the huge number of visitors. After wet weather the zigzagging forest path gets very muddy, so choose appropriate footwear. The monastery is 1,250m above sea level, and though the path only climbs through 250m of these, the total distance of the path is 1,100m with 25 zigzags.

Behind its imposing 18th-century façade, the monastery is in ruins as a result of a fire earlier this century. Founded in the 6th century, the last monks only left in 1923 when all Greeks in Turkey went back to Greece in an 'exchange of populations'. Though severely defaced and covered in graffiti, many of the remaining frescos are still very fine, notably the Adam and Eve series.
48km south of Trabzon. Open: daily, 8am–5pm. Admission charge.

BLACK SEA COAST

The defaced interior of the Sumela Monastery

TRABZON (TREBIZOND)

The days when fabled Trebizond lay like a 'green Eden' at the foot of the Pomtic mountains, a little Constantinople on the Black Sea, are long past, and you have to go in search of Trabzon's towers and fine monuments. That said, as long as you arrive with realistic expectations, Trabzon does offer some interest.

Its relics today are its churches, dating from the time when Trabzon was capital of a Byzantine dynasty called

Comnene, which survived here some 250 years, the emperor's son Comnenus having fled Constantinople when it fell in the Fourth Crusade in 1204. Trabzon's most famous relic is the Aya Sofya Cathedral on the outskirts of town, now a museum. The Ottomans converted it to a mosque in the 15th century, whitewashing the walls, and the rescue of the frescos underneath took six years in the 1950s. Besides this cathedral, the other buildings to look for in the town centre are St Anna, St Andrew and the Fatih Camii in the citadel area. At the summit of the citadel, a few walls of the Comnene palace remain. Ask for *kale* (castle). On the outskirts of town, Atatürk's Summer House and museum are site's of pilgrimage for many Turks.

365km east of Samsun, 250km west of Artvin and 322km northwest of Erzurum. Aya Sofya Cathedral open: Tuesday to Sunday, 8.30am–noon and 1pm–5pm. Admission charge.

VAN

The whole Van area was closed to visitors before 1960. Today it is eastern Turkey's most forward-looking town, with a university and several training schools. It lies 4km away from the lakeshore, and in the modern town itself the only place of interest to the visitor is the small but well-presented museum (open: Tuesday to Sunday, 9am–noon and 1pm–5.30pm; admission charge) with a superb display of Urartian gold jewellery.

Van served for 300 years as capital to the little-known Urartian empire, successors to the Hittites and similar to them in looks and in language. They were distinguished builders, favouring long thin spurs as sites for their fortress cities and there are over 30 such fortresses scattered over their empire, the largest being Van Kalesi and Çavuştepe. Their most impressive skill was metalwork, in which they led the world. Urartian-worked gold, silver and bronze was exported westwards and evidence is mounting that the ancient Greeks and Etruscans copied heavily from Urartian originals.

Van is 402km northeast of Diyarbakır and 147km east of Tatvan.

The remains of Ottoman Van, with the Rock of Van in the background

Van Kalesi (Van Castle)

On the lakeshore 4km west of the modern town stands this extraordinary Rock of Van, the Urartian citadel. It is a freak outcrop 2km long and 100m high, that dominates the flat plain all around. One 19th-century traveller described it as 'a kneeling camel in profile'. On the thin narrow summit follow the paths to discover the colossal 8th- and 9th-century BC rock-cut tombs of the Urartian kings and a temple, as well as some crumbling Ottoman buildings. In Ottoman times Van castle was a military base and up to 3,000 Janissaries and soldiers lived here.

Down below, your eye will be drawn by the ruins of a few isolated mosques. This is all that remains of the Ottoman city of Old Van which once had one of the largest populations in Anatolia, two-thirds of which was Armenian. Its total destruction by the Turks after World War I is still a subject of controversy.

VAN ENVIRONS

Akdamar Island, see pages 136–7.

Çavuştepe

The second largest Urartian citadel after Van Kalesi, Çavuştepe lies on the road to Hakkari. Here you can explore a temple, and a royal palace, still impressive for the beautifully carved blocks.
Open: daily, 8.30am–sunset. Admission charge.

Güzelsu (Hoşap)

The best example of a Kurdish castle to be seen in Turkey today, Hoşap looks, with its crenellated battlements and turrets, as if it has been lifted straight from a fairy tale, perched up on its own

The Castle of Hosap at Güzelsu. Built in 1643 to such impressive design, a legend arose that the architect's hands were severed to prevent him from repeating the work elsewhere

ill. You can drive right up to the impressive entrance gate. The interior is surprisingly open and grassy. In its heyday it is known to have had 360 rooms and two mosques.

48km east of Van on the Hokkari road. Open: daily, 8.30am–sunset. Admission charge.

Hakkari

There are no specific monuments to visit in this extreme southeastern corner of Turkey, but the journey down here from Van is worthwhile for the magnificent scenery which begins at the Zab valley. In the past, foreigners ventured here for the superb mountaineering in the peaks east of Hakkari and south of Yüksekova. With the problem of Kurdish insurgency however, climbing in the Hakkari region has been forbidden, and until the political situation is more settled, you would be advised to stick to the main routes and certainly to avoid heading up small tracks into villages..
204km south of Van.

Van Gölü (Lake Van), see pages 136–7.

A Drive Through the Georgian Valleys

This tour takes you from Erzurum on the eastern Anatolian plateau northwards through the beautiful Georgian valleys of the Tortum and Çoruh rivers, then over the Karçal mountains down to the Black Sea coast at Hopa. Besides the magnificently verdant mountain scenery, you can visit several churches of the Georgian Christians who used to live in these valleys, now in use as mosques or storerooms. A fairly remote and thinly populated region, it is advisable to take your own provisions along and to set out with a full tank

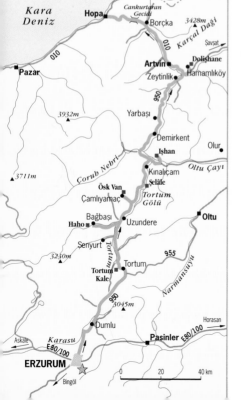

of petrol. *The total distance is 283km and you should regard it as a leisurely day's drive. If you want to explore the region more thoroughly, you can break the journey at Artvin, set high in the mountains, where there is reasonable accommodation.*

It is after Tortum, 50km to the north of Erzurum, that the scenery becomes interesting, as you enter a narrowing gorge with the Tortum river running through it. The derelict Tortum Kale (castle) is visible on a clifftop to the left but access is difficult. Beside an arched bridge over the river 25km beyond Tortum, a battered yellow plaque announces Bağbası, the village 8km up the drivable track to the left, where the 10th-century church of Haho lies.

BAĞBASI

The Georgians are a Caucasian race, separate from the Turks, and some 50,000 of them still survive in Turkey in these remote valleys, many recognisable by their ginger hair and freckles. As an outpost of Christianity in Asia, the

Georgian family preparing apples to dry in the sun at Ishan

egion was singled out by the Mongol
'amerlane for heavy attacks, leaving
owns and villages in ruins.

The church of Haho lies some 300m
beyond the village centre, and now
erves as the community mosque.

*Back on the main road you continue north
further 15km until you notice a sign to
Çamlıyamaç, up an earth road to the left.*

ÇAMLIYAMAÇ

In the heart of this village stands the vast
shell of Ösk Van monastery church.
Dating from the 11th century, there are
some fine paintings in the porch, with
reliefs adorning the façade.

*The drive now becomes very dramatic,
spiralling above the left cliffside of Tortum
Gölü (Lake Tortum)
Fork right 35km north of the Ösk Van*

*turn-off, towards Olur. Seven kilometres
later, an earth road winds up 9km to reach
Işhan.*

IŞHAN

This is the home of the third of the
Georgian churches. The church stands
in a lovely setting. The windows bear
fine carvings and some 11th-century
murals are still preserved.

*From Işhan, rejoin the main road heading
north until you reach the right turn for the
village of Hamamlıköy on the Şavşat road.
Here you will find the fourth and final
Georgian church, Dolışhane.
You now head towards Artvin on the upper
valley slopes.
From Artvin to Hopa the road snakes
through heavily wooded hills, descending
through the lush tea plantations which
characterise this coast.*

Lake Van Drive

This lake circuit is probably the most picturesque and relaxing of any drive in eastern Turkey. The roads are easy and traffic-free, the places to see along the way are uncrowded, and all are in isolated locations outside towns. It also incorporates a visit to the tiny Akdamar Adası (Akdamar Island), justly famous for its solitary Armenian church, covered in stone-carved biblical reliefs. *The whole circuit is a distance of 322km and takes a whole day, but if you only have half a day, restrict yourself to Akdamar.*

Setting off from Van south towards Gevaş, after 47km there is a yellow sign announcing Akdamar beside a little ferry landing stage. A restaurant and picnic area are to the left of the road.

For boats to take you the 2km across to Akdamar Island, you should always arrive in the morning, and it is best to avoid weekends, when it becomes a popular picnic site for Turkish families. In season (May to October), boats which can carry up to 50 people are waiting at the landing stage to take fare-paying visitors across. Out of season, it is a lot more expensive as you have to hire a boat for yourself.

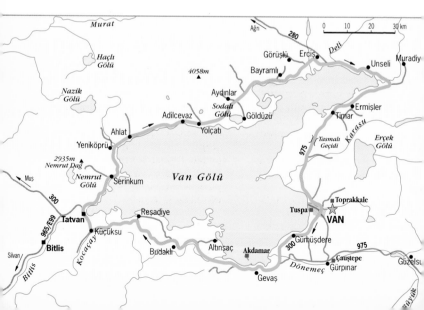

AKDAMAR ISLAND

After disembarking, climb the stepped path up to the terrace where the Church of the Holy Cross stands, a masterpiece of early Armenian art, the cathedral church of the independent Armenian kingdom of Vaspurakan. Armenia was the first country to adopt Christianity as the state religion in AD280. This church, built in 915 by King Gagik I, is still in astonishingly good condition, especially considering it has never been restored. The stone carved reliefs are quite comic, notably Jonah and the Whale, David and Goliath and Abraham and Isaac.

The grassy island makes a good picnic spot and you can even find a pebbly beach to swim from, in the wonderfully clear silky waters of the lake. Six times saltier than the sea, even the most leaden of people can float.

After the return ferry trip continue westwards towards Tatvan, where the road leaves the lake for a while to zigzag up a high pass with lovely mountain scenery of bubbling streams and flowering meadows. From Tatvan follow the yellow sign marked Nemrut which leads northwards out of the town.

NEMRUT

This refers to the volcano Nemrut Dağı, whose summit at almost 3,000m, is only accessible in July and August when the snow melts. A rough path leads to the crater rim and, for the energetic, even down inside (see pages 144–5).

The lakeside road arrives next at Ahlat.

AHLAT

The village is known today for its extensive Seljuk cemetery of tall

The silky waters of Lake Van

tombstones and its large *kümbets*, tall conical tombs. These are scattered about the town, easily spotted in the flat landscape, and are best driven round.

The shoreline between Ahlat and Adilcevaz has lovely stretches of deserted beach to swim and picnic.

ADILCEVAZ

At the pretty village of Adilcevaz you can visit the chocolate-coloured mosque on the lakeshore, then climb up to the Seljuk castle on the steep outcrop behind, for fine views over the still lake.

Twenty kilometres east of Adilcevaz you come to Sodalı Gölü, a freshwater lake where lots of birds come to fish.

The final stretch of the drive, through the village of Erciş back to Van, offers yet more attractive lake scenery.

WATER: THE FUTURE OF THE EUPHRATES

Water is unquestionably the resource of the coming decade, and Turkey has it in abundance. The sources of both the Dicle (Tigris) and the Firat (Euphrates) lie high in the Anatolian mountains, so Turkey can turn the tap on and off at will.

The Southeast Anatolia Project (known as GAP) is Turkey's vision of the future. The most ambitious scheme ever undertaken by any country in the region, it consists of a series of 22 dams on the Upper Euphrates to transform an area of wasteland in the southeast the size of the Benelux countries, back into fertile agricultural land – Mesopotamia reborn. Turkey is the only state in the region which has the labour, land and infrastructure to develop large-scale agriculture and food-processing.

The massive Atatürk Dam opened in 1992 is the centrepiece of the project, 60km north of Urfa. The Tigris will be used mainly for generating hydroelectric power, and there will eventually be 19 hydroelectric power plants which will ensure Turkey's self-sufficiency.

The project also has social engineering objectives, as the area affected is populated by semi-nomadic Kurds engaged in sheep-rearing. The Turkish government estimates that work will be created for hundreds of thousands of agricultural workers in the cotton and cereal fields and hopes that the advent of economic prosperity will calm the social unrest.

Syria and Iraq are of course somewhat less inspired by Turkey's vision. In 1990 they had to suffer a month of greatly reduced flow while Turkey diverted water to fill the Atatürk reservoir.

The Atatürk Dam

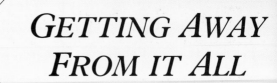

GETTING AWAY FROM IT ALL

'For once seen, never can the magnificent sight of the "Queen of the Cities" rising out of the sparkling waters of the Bosphorus be forgotten, with its seven hills crowned with great domed mosques surrounded by tapering minarets, with marble palaces, built in tiers down to the water's edge of the Sea of Marmara and Golden Horn...'
LADY DORINA NEAVE (1890)

Boat Trips

NORTHERN CYPRUS

If you are holidaying on Turkey's Mediterranean coast and want to get away to a different country, you could take a boat from Alanya or Taşucu to Girne (Kyrenia) in the northern Turkish part of Cyprus. No visas are required, fares are cheap and the boats (passengers only) run several times a week taking about five hours from Taşucu and eight hours from Alanya. Tickets can be bought at the docks without advance booking. A car ferry also runs weekly from Mersin to Gazimağusa (Famagusta). North Cyprus is remarkably unspoilt and uncrowded, with lovely scenery and beaches. Car hire is cheap, so you can explore Crusader castles, classical monasteries and Greek monasteries all within short drives of each other. Kyrenia itself makes the best base and has a very pretty harbour with excellent restaurants. The currency is the Turkish lira and cars drive on the left, a leftover of British administration. (See page 81.)

RHODES

From Marmaris ferries run daily except Sundays to the Greek island of Rhodes taking two and a half hours. Boats at Marmaris harbour also offer numerous day trips to neighbouring bays with fish barbecues on deserted beaches. A stroll along the harbourfront examining the various placards will tell the range and the prices.

A day or so spent exploring the

GÜLET CRUISING

Gülets are the traditional motor yachts that have been built for generations from the red pine that grows in abundance all over Turkey's southern shore. This coastline is increasingly becoming associated with *gület* holidays, where visitors spend their seven or 14 days cruising in leisurely fashion from bay to bay, dropping anchor for a swim here, exploring an ancient city ruin there. Most boats sleep eight to 12 people, and the Turkish crew sees to all the catering and the route, so all you have to do is sit back and relax. Space is limited on board so minimalist packing is called for. Most cabins have a private toilet and shower with hot water provided by the on-board generator. The boats are very attractive, with a shaded area on deck, and many have a cassette recorder so you can bring your own tapes. Children under 12 are not accepted, except if the whole boat has been booked by one party. Marmaris, Bodrum, Fethiye, Kalkan and Kas are the main centres, but there are many more small fishing villages to call off at along the way. Holidays combining seven days' *gület* cruising with seven days on shore are becoming very popular. On a 14 day cruise it is possible to motor all the way from Bodrum to Fethiye, and transport is then arranged to get you back to the airport. Your local Turkish Tourist Office can supply you with a list of the many tour operators who specialise in *gület* cruising.

walled Crusader town of Rhodes can be very pleasant, but it is best to avoid high season (July and August), when it can get very crowded.

Other Greek islands which are an easy hop from the Turkish mainland are Lesbos (reached from Ayvalık), Khios (from Çeşme), Samos (from Kuşadası), and Kos (from Bodrum). In all cases, ferries run regularly and fares are reasonable. Tickets can be bought on the harbourfronts and no visas are required.

A family holiday aboard a traditional *gület* motor yacht

The Lakes

To escape the crowds, especially during public holidays when the beach resorts tend to be packed to bursting, it is worth remembering these fresh-water lakes, which lie just a short drive inland from Antalya. They offer excellent swimming in a peaceful environment, with a few simple hotels and pensions.

BEYŞEHIR

This lake is good for swimming and has an interesting mosque and *türbe* (1298) right on the shore. There are several pleasant restaurants along the river outlet of the lake. North of Beyşehir town on the Isparta road a track leads up 21km to the enigmatic Hittite sanctuary of Elflatunpınarı with fine carved reliefs *in situ*, but submerged in a pond.

EĞRIDIR

This is the loveliest of the western lakes, the trees and greenery round its shores making a welcome change from the bleak Anatolian plateau. As the altitude is 1,000m, the lake water is cold except in the height of summer, but its clarity and blueness are so inviting that the desire to immerse yourself in it is likely to get the better of you. The mountain setting is exquisite, and the little town of Eğridir itself offers reasonable accommodation and restaurants, with white bass and baby crayfish a lake speciality.

The town is situated on a little promontory jutting out into the lake, and the remains of a Seljuk castle on this promontory enclose an extraordinary series of old Turkish houses perched in precarious positions on the edge. Mixed in with them are old Greek houses, now derelict, and a Greek basilica with its roof still intact testifies to the size of the Greek community that lived here before the 1923 exchange of populations. A pebble-built causeway now links the promontory with two little islands.

At Barla on the lakeshore to the north there is a mosque with an attractively tiled minaret, and the drive there takes you past some of the best swimming spots.

South of Eğridir an excursion of 25km takes you to the very pretty Kovada National Park centred on an alpine lake dotted with islands, where there is lovely forest walking.

EASTERN LAKES

Turkey's eastern lakes offer vast expanses of silent water, not fresh, but salty water full of minerals. Tuz Gölü is somewhere just passed *en route* to somewhere else, but Van offers an extraordinarily rich variety of lakeshore sights (see pages 132–3, and pages 136–7), as well as the beauty of the lake and its surrounding mountains.

TUZ GÖLÜ (GREAT SALT LAKE)

Remarkable for its sheer size, this great salt lake lies on the road from Ankara to Aksaray on the edge of Cappadocia, a shimmering expanse devoid of life. There are special parking areas where you can get down to the shoreline to touch the crusty edge.

VAN

Turkey's biggest lake and seven times bigger than Lake Geneva, the colossal Lake Van has a quality that verges on

ishermen checking their nets on a tranquil Lake Eğridir

he eerie. The piercing blue water lies
,750m above sea level, and is itself
inged with peaks rising to 3,000m and
ven 4,000m, snow-covered for all but
uly and August. Its aspects change with
he season and from different points on
he shore. Some stretches are gaunt and
are while others are colourful with
lowers and trees. The lake was formed
y the eruption of Nemrut Dağı aeons
go, forming a huge dam of lava that
locked the outflow. Several small rivers
low into the lake, but there is no
utflow. Its level stays constant,
owever, through evaporation. This
henomenon is the reason why the water
as become highly alkaline with natural
odas. Fishermen simply trail their dirty
vashing behind their boats to get a

whiter than white wash! It also leaves a
smooth feeling on the skin, making
swimming a very pleasurable experience.
 There is good accommodation in
Tatvan and Van, and you can travel
between the two on the ferry which
makes the link for the railway. The
whole train drives on to the ferry!

SPAS

Besides the lakes, Turkey also has
about 1,000 thermal springs. Spas
with facilities for therapeutic treatment
are: Balçova, Balıklı, Bolu, Bursa,
Çermik, Çesme, Gönen, Harlek,
Hüdanya, Ilgin, Karahayıt,
Kızılcahamam, Pamukkale, Sakar
and Yalova.

Mountains and Treks

BÜYÜKAĞRI DAĞI (MOUNT ARARAT)

At 5,165m Ararat is Turkey's highest peak. In summer the snow line retreats to the top third, while in winter it comes right down to the plateau, itself at 1,800m. The usual ascent route takes three days from the base camp of Doğubeyazıt, with one or two days for the descent. It is not a technically difficult climb, but requires great stamina. Most ascents take place in June, July and August. Sudden changes in weather are the mountain's speciality, and people have been killed in the ascent. The jagged lava fields covered in ice near the summit require the use of an ice-axe and crampons. The most recent eruption was in 1840. The small cone of Little Ararat stands beside the

Trekking in Lycia

big one like a child beside its parent.

Armenian tradition has Ararat as the centre of the universe, and the Bible cites Ararat as the place where Noah's Ark came to rest after the Flood. Expeditions are regularly mounted to try to locate the elusive Ark.

CAPPADOCIA

This is good rambling terrain, and Cappadocia's typical rock-cut churches and natural caves form excellent shelter at night. Donkeys are used for porterage. Gradients are easy and only normal fitness is required. The myriad rough tracks also lend themselves to horse-riding, and several tour operators offer seven day treks. (See pages 162–3.)

KAÇKAR

Also known as the Little Caucasus, this is the mountain range inland from the

ORGANISED TREKKING AND MOUNTAINEERING

Usually involving groups of 10 to 15, these are becoming increasingly popular, with Mount Ararat and the Kaçkar range presenting a serious challenge to stamina (though not requiring previous experience) in the eastern half of the country, while the Taurus mountains of Lycia in the west are more like hilly country walking. Your local Tourist Office will supply you with a list of the tour operators who specialise in these holidays. Donkeys usually carry baggage and supplies, and accommodation is a mixture of hotels and camping.

ttoman bridge at Çamlıhemsin in the Kaçkar mountains

lack Sea between Rize and Pazar. The
arting point for climbs is Çamlıhemsin,
om where the route is up through lush
mi-tropical vegetation, through the
gh *yaylas* (summer pastures) to the
eaks around 3,500m. Once on the
her side, the going is drier with bleaker
rrain. The midsummer months are
est when days are mild and nights cold.

ÖPRÜLÜ

his canyon leading up to the Central
aurus mountains is a popular 10-day
ke, ending at Eğridir and its lake (see
ages 142–3, and pages 98–9).

LYCIA

There are many hikes in Lycia's inland
mountains, often spending the night in
remote villages up on the high *yaylas*,
where the local people bring their flocks
to pasture in the summer, to escape the
heat of the coast.

The walks tend to follow mule tracks
and usually incorporate a few ruined
Lycian cities on the way. Scenery is
spectacular, and though hilly, your
fitness level need be only moderate, with
four to six hours' walking a day. The
best times are May and June, September
and October.

National Parks

*T*urkey is a country blessed with huge tracts of virgin landscape and these have been preserved in recent years by the creation of many national parks. All are in heavily forested areas, often with lakes and rivers, and are rich in flora and wildlife. They are all open to the public and are free of charge.

AEGEAN REGION

Kuş Cenneti Milli Parki (Bird Paradise)
A bird sanctuary just inland from the Sea of Marmara. *60km west of Bursa.*

Sipildağı Milli Parki
A National Park where one can see the famous 'crying rock' of Niobe. *20km northeast of Izmir on the Manisa road.*

Uludağ Milli Parki
A heavily forested area round Uludağ, the ancient Mount Olympos. In winter is a busy ski resort, but in summer it is rich with mountain walks amid streams and wild flowers (see pages 48–9, and 162–3). *35km east of Bursa.*

MEDITERRANEAN REGION

Beydaglari Olimpos Milli Parki
This incorporates the ancient ruins of

FLORA AND FAUNA
The national parks have allowed Turkey's rich flora and fauna to flourish in a protected environment, but many colourful flowers also grow wild on the hillsides and even on the roadsides in the Aegean and Mediterranean regions. April and May are the most impressive months, when the pink oleander bushes, red anenomes and poppies, and white irises abound. Tumbling white jasmine and purple bourgainvillea continue to bloom throughout the summer in many gardens. The Turks adore flowers and are inspired gardeners specialising in the 'chaotic profusion' look.

In the western regions, the main form of wildlife encountered is the mosquito, though they are no worse than any other Mediterranean country. From April until September many types of butterfly can be found feeding on the flowers, but the rarer species like the white admiral and purple emperor are to be found inland rather than on the coast. Scorpions and snakes are not abundant but do exist, so it is worth being careful if walking on rougher ground with bare ankles and legs. In the Aegean coastal areas it is common to see tortoises strolling across the less trafficked roads.

Along the roadsides on the southern Mediterranean, large hairy, two-humped camels are still to be seen, giving way in Central Anatolia to the huge black water buffalo, with their long beards and fierce horns. Both are used as beasts of burden. Sheep, goats and cattle are plentiful. In the remoter more mountainous areas to the east, bears, badgers, boar, deer, ibex, jackals and gazelles can be seen, together with wild cats, wolves, wild dogs and even leopards in the forests.

Olympos, and lies just inland from Kemer (see page 92). *20km south of Antalya.*

Güllükdağı Milli Parki
This is the park around the ancient city of Termessos high in the mountains (see pages 84–5). *34km northwest of Antalya, off E24 towards Korkuteli.*

Kizildağ Milli Parki
A beautiful park of cedar trees situated on the northwestern fringe of Lake Beyşehir. *North of Antalya.*

Kovada Gölü Milli Parki
Centred on a lake in the mountains. *25km south of Lake Eğridir, inland from Antalya.*

Köprülü Kanyon Milli Parki
On the way to the ruins of Selge. *60km north of Side* (see pages 98–9).

CENTRAL REGION

Boğazkale-Alacahöyük Milli Parki
This incorporates the ancient Hittite sites of Boğazkale and Alacahöyük. *East of Ankara.*

Çamlık Milli Parki
Famous for its king eagles, this park is adjacent to Yozgat. *40km south of Boğazkale.*

Göreme Milli Parki
This incorporates the Göreme valley and its rock-cut churches in Cappadocia.

EASTERN REGION AND THE BLACK SEA

Altındere Milli Parki
This incorporates the Sumela monastery. *45km inland from Trabzon on the Black Sea coast.*

Ilgaz Milli Parki
This lies 45km south of Kastamonu, inland from Inebolu on the Black Sea.

A stork constructing its nest, a familiar sight in many parts of Turkey

Karatepe Milli Parki
The park is situated on the Cayhan River valley in Adana province and incorporates the ancient Hittite site of Karatepe. *100km northeast of Adana.*

Munzur Vadisi Milli Parki
One of the wildest areas of Turkey where bears are still found. *50km south of Erzincan, near Ovacık.*

Nemrut Dağı Milli Parki
This incorporates the famous mountaintop heads on Nemrut Dağı. *60km south of Malatya.*

Soğuksu Milli Parki
This lies 110km inland from Zonguldak on the Black Sea coast.

Yedigöller Milli Parki
Magnificent scenery with seven lakes, excellent trekking terrain. *50km inland from Zonguldak on the Black Sea coast.*

Birdwatching

*A*rmed with a pair of binoculars and a field guide (such as *The Birds of Britain and Europe with North Africa and the Middle East* by Heinzel, Fitter and Parslow), you can add a whole new dimension to your holiday.

While there are specialist tour operators who offer birdwatching holidays, birdwatching in Turkey is by and large something you can combine with your own sightseeing or even with lazing on the beach. Turkey offers a remarkably wide range of birdlife due to its geographical position on the edge of Europe, Asia and Africa. Birds from all three continents are to be found here, and the unusually wide range of climatic conditions adds to the diversity. In spring and summer there is the added attraction of two major north-south migration routes. These migrations are on a huge scale: nearly 400,000 birds of prey have been recorded passing the northwest Black Sea coast in one season.

May is probably the best birdwatching month, and on a typical

Booted eagle with young

two- to three-week touring holiday, the inexperienced birdwatcher can be assured of spotting well over 100 species. Large distinctive birds which anyone will notice are the tall storks whose enormous nests are often to be seen on minarets, rooftops and telegraph poles. Around rivers and lakes grey herons are also difficult to miss. Overhead, vultures and birds of prey are common, if not always readily identifiable, and the bird which is always running off the tarmac and flying up under the wheels is the crested lark.

Turkey boasts several bird sanctuaries, notably Kuş Cenneti in Marmara, and at Birecik on the Syrian border, where the bald ibis, a large and extraordinary bird on the verge of extinction, is the subject of a World Wildlife Rescue Operation.

For more information contact The Ornithological Society of the Middle East, c/o The Lodge, Sandy, Bedfordshire SG19 2DL England.

Great egret

DIRECTORY

'If God wants to make
a poor man happy, he
makes him lose his
donkey and
then find it again.'
TURKISH PROVERB

Shopping

*T*urkey offers an unusually large variety of souvenirs, and most people are pleasantly surprised by the high standard and good value. In bazaars, bargaining is the norm, and even when prices are marked, you should aim to knock around one-third off the first quoted price. As a rule the longer you are prepared to spend bargaining, the better the deal you get. In normal shops like pharmacies, grocers, clothes boutiques and so on, the prices are fixed, so there is no point trying to bargain over a packet of aspirin. Normal shopping hours are 9.30am–1pm and 2pm–7pm, closed Sundays. The Covered Bazaar is open 8.30am–7pm, closed Sundays.

ISTANBUL

Istanbul is the shopping highpoint in Turkey, and nobody should miss the Covered Bazaar (see pages 50–1), where virtually every souvenir made even in Turkey's most distant corners, such as knitted socks from Erzurum, can be found under the same roof.

Spices for sale

THE COVERED BAZAAR

An exhaustive list is not possible, but among the main items you will find in the Bazaar are:

Alabaster: a translucent calcite or gypsum, made into chess sets, eggcups, ashtrays etc.

Antiques: many genuine but even more fake. Export of antiques is strictly forbidden and carries a stiff prison sentence. If you buy something old, get the shop-owner to state the age on the invoice and make sure he signs it.

Camel-bone boxes: beautifully hand painted.

Carpets: an apparently infinite selection of carpets and *kilims* at good prices (see pages 74–5).

Ceramics: colourful abstract and floral designs on Islamic motifs, usually in blues and greens, made into jugs, pots, plates, bowls and tiles.

Copper and brassware: a brass tea tray with carrying handle and tea glasses makes an unusual and usable souvenir. Copper is toxic, so should not be used for eating and drinking vessels unless coated with tin on the inside, something which is cheap and easy to have done here.

Denim: vast quantities of all kinds of denim clothing, and also cheap canvas

Corner grocer in Istanbul's old quarter

bags in all sizes to carry home your purchases.

Gold and silver: the daily gold price is chalked up on a blackboard on Kuyumcular Caddesi, the Street of the Jewellers. The silver *han* (Kalcılar Hanı) has an amazing variety, and pieces can be made to order here in just a few days.

Jewellery: an extraordinary selection, often using semi-precious stones like turquoise, amethyst, garnet, onyx, jade and lapis lazuli.

Leather and suede: all different shapes and sizes of coats, jackets, skirts, trousers, shoes, bags, and belts. The leather is beautifully soft, but any purchase needs to be carefully inspected to check workmanship and exact sizing.

Spices: the whole range from ginger to curry, sold from open sacks, also at the Spice Market (Misir Carşışı) beside Yeni Cami, Eminönü.

Turkish delight: known as *lokum*, which comes in flavours like lemon, mint or pistachio, packed and presented in every conceivable variety and quantity.

HOW TO BUY A CARPET

1 Stick to Turkish pieces. While Iranian, Caucasian and Turcoman are available, they are often more expensive in Turkey than elsewhere due to rarity value.
2 Check closeness of weave by looking at the back. The closer the weave, the smaller the knot, the higher the price. Wet a handerchief and rub it over to check colour fastness, and look carefully for repairs.
3 To check silk is not synthetic, put a match to the fringe. Real silk does not flame easily, while the synthetic glows and has a chemical smell.
(See also **Shopping**, pages 150–3.)

Carpets stacked for sale

Benetton and **Lacoste** also have shops here.

For food, the famous places are the **Fish Market** (Balıkpazarı) on Istiklal Caddesi, Galatasaray, Beyoğlu, and the **Egyptian Spice Bazaar** (Misir Çarşışı) for spices, sweets and Turkish delight. **Migros** in Şişli district is the biggest supermarket, and **Printemps** at the Galleria Ataköy shopping mall on the airport road, is the best department store.

The larger hotels in Istanbul and indeed throughout Turkey, have their own souvenir shops often with very high quality goods, if somewhat expensive, but nevertheless very convenient for those short of time.

SPECIAL INTEREST SHOPPING

Arasta Bazaar
Behind the Blue Mosque, Sultanahmet, a street of souvenir shops converted from the Ottoman sultan's stables, selling carpets, *kilims*, jewellery and brassware, at prices a little higher than the Covered Bazaar.

Beyazıt Sahaflar Çarşışı
The book market between the Covered Bazaar and the Beyazıt Mosque, excellent for all books new and old in all languages. Also good for calendars and Turkish miniatures.

Istanbul Handicrafts Centre
Beside the Yeşil Ev Hotel, Sultanahmet, where you can watch artisans at work and buy their creations.

FOOD AND CLOTHING
For fashion clothing, **Beymen** is the top quality chain of Turkish-made men's and women's wear. A new children's range has just been launched. Ask your hotel reception for the nearest branch.

ISTANBUL ENVIRONS
Bursa has a covered bazaar (*bedestan*) in the town centre, where the best buys are towels, knives and silk.

AEGEAN REGION

Bodrum
The main bazaar area is round the foot of the castle with shops selling wide selections of rugs, embroidery, copperware, sponges and lapis lazuli beads to ward off the 'evil eye'. Leisure clothes made of soft cotton also make a very attractive buy.

Dalyan
Has a small range of souvenir shops in the town.

Kuşadası
Has a large and lively bazaar offering the full range of souvenirs.

Izmir
Has a covered market just inland from the clock tower on the seafront.

Marmaris
The best shopping is in the renovated Ottoman *caravanserai* (Kervanseray).

MEDITERRANEAN REGION
The big cities of **Adana**, **Antalya** and **Antakya** all have covered bazaars in their centres. Fethiye has a bustling daily food market as well as lots of souvenir shops.

The resort villages of **Kalkan**, **Kaş**, **Kemer** and **Side** offer a sophisticated range of souvenir shops, including carpets and *kilim* shops, with lots of small bright shops clustered in narrow streets.

CENTRAL REGION

Ankara
The city is not blessed with exciting or even abundant souvenir shops, so save your shopping for elsewhere.
Kayseri
A noted centre of the carpet trade, and many souvenir and jewellery shops now exist in the renovated citadel and bazaar areas.

Konya
A well-known carpet centre. The souvenir shops are all in the centre, clustered near the Mevlana Tekke.
Ürgüp
This Cappadocia town has an excellent range of shops on its main street opposite the museum, selling silver jewellery and semi-precious stones, and nomad knitwear. Cappadocia is generally well-provided with souvenir shops. Avanos is famous for its red pottery made from the local red clay.

EASTERN REGION AND THE BLACK SEA
Souvenir shops are few and far between in eastern Turkey and on the Black Sea coast. Among the best buys available are carpets, nomad multi-coloured knitted gloves and socks, and embroidered headscarves. In **Erzurum** the local black jet (*oltu*) is made into various artefacts such as worry beads and necklaces, on sale in the vicinity of the Ulu Cami.

Typical, highly coloured Turkish ceramic plates on display

Entertainment

*T*hroughout Turkey, the most commonly indulged form of entertainment is eating out, or drinking tea and coffee in bars and cafés watching the world go by or playing backgammon. Istanbul has the lion's share of the country's organised entertainment. Elsewhere there is little except discos in the resorts and all cultural activity is concentrated on the annual festivals such as the Bodrum Culture and Art Week and the Antalya Film and Art Festival. Cinema and theatre are currently undergoing a revival, especially in Istanbul, and the Atatürk Cultural Centres in Istanbul, Ankara and Izmir, Turkey's three main cities, offer classical music, ballet and operatic performances. There are nightclubs presenting special shows with belly dancing and folk dancing, where the clientele is almost exclusively non-Turkish. Traditional Turkish dance and music are to be found in the annual festivals like the Istanbul International Art and Culture Festival in June and July (see pages 158-9). Discos are ubiquitous and usually good. Large city hotels sometimes have casinos and discos, all have bars and all have TV and in-house video. Turkish TV has a number of English shows and films, and the week's programmes are listed in the *Turkish Daily News*, Turkey's only English language daily paper. Listings for cinema and theatre are occasionally given in the paper too, but more often you will have to ask or look out for adverts and posters.

ISTANBUL

BARS AND CAFÉS

All the major hotels have bars and cafés where non-residents are welcome. The following are particularly popular with Istanbul residents.

Les Ambassadeurs

A piano bar with luxurious atmosphere and fabulous Bosphorus views. *Swissôtel, Maçka (tel: 259 01 01). Open: 11pm–1.30am.*

Bebek Bar

In the leafy residential area of Bebek with a terrace overlooking the sea. Try the white cheese. *Cevdet Paşa Caddesi 15, Bebek (tel: 263 30 00). Open: 7pm–1am.*

Beyaz Köşk (White Pavilion)

In the grounds of the charming Emirgan Park in a restored 17th-century building, serving cakes, sandwiches and drinks. *Emirgan (tel: 277 70 61).*

Cabaret Çine

Recommended for its Bosphorus views, its stews and its live music. *Yeşilpinar Sokak 2, Arnavutköy (tel: 257 74 28).*

Çadır Köşku

Set in the lovely Yıldız Park, serving cakes and hotel drinks. *Yıldız Park, Beşiktaş (tel: 260 07 09). Open: 9am–6pm.*

Café Saray

In the newly restored Çırağan Palace with a lovely summer terrace overlooking the Bosphorus. *Çırağan Palace Hotel Kempinksi, Çırağan (tel: 258 33 77).*

Gezi

Serves Middle European pastries with a backdrop of classical music. *Inönü Caddesi 5/1, Taksim (tel: 251 74 30). Open: 7.30am–9pm.*

Myott Café

The in-place for local yuppies, also

popular with foreigners for wholesome breakfasts of muesli and fresh fruit. Music. *Iskele Sokak 14, Ortaköy. Open: 9am–4pm.*

Orient Bar
The bar and café of this well-known hotel. *Pera Palas Hotel, Tepebaşı (tel: 251 45 60). Open: 10.30pm–2am.*

Pierre Loti Café
Set in the house where the late 19th-century French poet and novelist lived, above the Eyüp graveyard overlooking the Golden Horn. (See pages 52–3.) Serves tea and coffee only. *Eyüp (tel: 581 26 96).*

Tonoz Bar
In the restored Sepetçiler Palace, now converted to an International Press Centre. Peaceful with good views. *Sepetçiler Kasrı, Kennedy Caddesi, Sarayburnu (tel: 511 45 03). Open: 8.30am–1am.*

Zindan Han
The building was a Byzantine and Ottoman prison, and now has good leather, jewellery and art shops, with a rooftop bar and restaurant. *Eminönü, next to Ticaret Odası (tel: 512 42 70).*

CASINOS
Büyük Surmeli Hotel, *Gayrettepe (tel: 272 11 60).*
Çırağan Palace Casino, *Çırağan Caddesi 84, Beşiktaş (tel: 259 63 00).*
Conrad Casino, *Conrad Hotel, Besiktaş (tel: 266 11 29).*
Grand Casino Bosphorus, *Swissôtel, Maçka (tel: 259 07 42).*

Mövenpick Casino, *Mövenpick Hotel, Maslak (tel: 285 09 00).*
Sheraton International Casino Club, *Taksim (tel: 246 20 21).*

CINEMAS
Most that show foreign films with Turkish subtitles are on Istiklal Caddesi in Beyoglu. They are Atlas, Beyoğlu, Dünya, Emek, Fitas, Lale and Cinepop. Always double check programmes and timings.

DISCOS
Andromeda
Acclaimed as one of the best-equipped clubs technically-speaking in the world, it has a gigantic 64 screen 'videowall', an amazing laser show, and a capacity of 2,000. Overheated fans jump into the pool in summer months. In winter it moves to its Taksim headquarters. *Gümüşyolu Caddesi, Nakkaştepe (tel: 310 53 95) (summer). Şan Müsikholü Arkası, Taksim (tel: 246 01 68) (winter).*

Taxim
This is a bar and restaurant with a dramatic disco on Fridays and Saturdays from 9pm till dawn. *Feridiye Mahallesi, Nizamiye Caddesi 12-16, Taksim (tel: 256 44 31).*

Folk dancer in Istanbul

All-male folk dance, Istanbul night club

EXHIBITIONS AND GALLERIES

Atatürk Cultural Centre, *Taksim (tel: 251 56 00)*. Shows a range of painting and other constantly changing exhibitions.

Baraz, *Kurtulus Caddesi 191, Kurtulus (tel: 240 47 83)*. Paintings of international and Turkish artists.

State Gallery of Fine Arts, *Istiklal Caddesi 209/49, Beyoğlu (tel: 243 90 53)*.

JAZZ CLUBS

Caz Bar, *Kourkent-levent (tel: 266 44 93)*.

Ece Bar, *Arnavutköy (tel: 265 96 01)*.

Kehribar, *Divan Hotel, Taksim (tel: 231 41 00)*.

MUSIC

The **Istanbul International Art and Culture Festival** in June and July includes jazz, ballet and orchestral music, as well as traditional Turkish music.

Istanbul Symphony Orchestra, *Atatürk Cultural Centre, Taksim (tel: 251 56 00)*. Entry to the orchestra's rehearsals on Fridays from 10.30am–1.30pm is free.

The Atatürk Cultural Centre is the state's showpiece for classical music, ballet, opera and theatre.

NIGHT CLUBS

Galata Tower Night Club
Belly dancing. *Karaköy (tel: 245 11 60)*.

Kervanseray
Belly dancing. *Elmadağ (tel: 247 16 30)*.

Orient House
Belly dancing and Turkish folk dancing. *Beyazıt (tel: 517 61 63)*.

Parisienne
Belly dancing, disco and bar. *Elmadağ (tel: 247 63 62)*.

Regine Revue
Belly dancing and floor show. *Elmadağ (tel: 246 74 49)*.

THEATRES

The theatre has been undergoing a renaissance in recent years and a number of new companies have been set up. Plays are sometimes performed in English, and programmes are listed in the *Turkish Daily News*.

ENTERTAINMENT IN ANKARA AND THE RESORTS

AEGEAN REGION

Bodrum

Veli is a 'live blues' bar on Dr Alim Bey

addesi. **Disco Halikarnas** on
umhuriyet Caddesi is probably the
rgest open-air disco in Europe.
xpensive, but with a free laser show
ointed at the castle.

zmir

urprisingly limited. There is the
tatürk Cultural Centre and the State
allet on Milli Kütüphane Caddesi, but
nly from late September until May.
he Izmir International Festival runs
aid-June to mid-July, but most events
re actually held either in Çeşme castle
r the Roman theatre at Ephesus.
rogramme and tickets from the Opera
nd Ballet box office, the museum in
elçuk or the Çeşme Tourist Office.

uşadası

Jightlife focuses on bars and discos, the
oisiest of which are **Fame Club** and
ted Bar on Kibris Caddesi. **Disco
'arisien** out of the islet has the best
etting.

Iarmaris

Iaxim's Disco on the Kordon is open
ntil 4am. **Palm Tree** on Haci Mustafa
okak 97 is like a garden pub with taped
nusic.

MEDITERRANEAN REGION

Antalya

Nightlife is concentrated on the yacht
arbour, where **Café Iskele** is
ttractively set round a fountain.
)therwise the only organised
ntertainment is during the Antalya
'estival (see pages 158–9).

'ethiye

Intel Club, a relaxed and friendly
iightclub opposite the Hotel Vizion.

Kaş
Odeon Café Bar is the best bar,
opposite Utopia bookshop. **Nokta
Redpoint** nightclub is just behind it.

Kemer
The larger hotels like the Kemer near
the marina have discos.

Side
Nimfeon Disco, on the way to the
eastern beach.

ANKARA AND CENTRAL
REGION

Ankara
The large hotels have discos and night
clubs. Ankara's best night club is the
Geceyarisi with a Turkish Oriental
and folklore group performing from
11pm until 5am. *Cinnan Caddesi No 5-
A (tel: 426 15 28).*
The State Symphony Orchestra and
State Opera and Ballet are based in
Ankara.

Ürgüp
Garden Compole on Istiklal Caddesi
has a folk-dancing programme, limitless
alcohol and an *à la carte* menu.
Harem Disco on Suat Hayri Ürgüplu
Caddesi.
Armagan Disco on Kayseri Caddesi.
The big hotels have discos, of which the
best is the Otel Mustafa, out of town on
the Kayseri road.

Avanos
Dragon *(tel: 4861/1486, 1506)* is the
best nightclub in the region, carved
from the soft rock, with the best belly
dancers.
Motif Restaurant *(tel: 4861/1577)* has
a good folk-dancing programme.

Festivals

January: Camel wrestling for most of the month throughout the province of Aydın. This unusual 'sport' involves two male camels pushing and shoving each other. While vicious, it is not usually a blood sport.

15–16 January: Camel wrestling festival at Selçuk, Ephesus Festival of Culture and Art with folk dancing, concerts and plays held in the Roman theatre of Ephesus.

May: Ankara International Arts Festival, to promote Turkey on an international level, with Turkish art, traditional Turkish classical music, and Turkish folklore music.

Last week of May: Pergamum Festival. Plays and folk dancing held in the Asklepieion theatre.

3–5 June: Aksaray Ihlara Folk Festival.

7–13 June: Music and Art Festival at Marmaris.

Last week of June: Artvin Kafkasör Culture and Art Festival, with bull fight on the Kafkasör plateau. Folkloric dancing and wrestling.

12 June–12 July: Bursa International Culture and Art Festival with folk dancing and music.

20 June–30 July: Istanbul International Art and Culture Festival with the full range of dance, art and music.

5–10 July: Aksehir Nasreddin Hoca Festival in honour of the famous wit, with plays of his anecdotes and folk dancing.

29–31 July: Foça, north of Izmir, Folklore and Watersports Festival.

1–25 August: Samsun Fair and Folkdance Festival.

15–18 August: Çanakkale Troy Festival, with folk dances, music, tours of Mount Ida and Troy.

The annual Selçuk Festival held in the ancient theatre at Ephesus

Children in traditional costume awaiting their turn in the folk dancing

20 August–20 September: Izmir International Fair. Amusements fair with cultural and commercial exhibitions. The city's hotels are packed and best avoided in this month.

1–9 September: Bodrum Culture and Art Week, with concerts in Bodrum Castle, local craft exhibits and watersports shows.

21–25 September: Cappadocia Festival, grape harvest celebration and folk dancing.

15 September–5 October: Mersin Fashion and Textile Show, with music and folklore.

October: Antalya Film and Art Festival, with some performances in the Roman theatre at Aspendos.

29 October: Republic Day, to commemorate the proclamation of the republic by Atatürk in 1923. Parades in the cities.

6–8 December: St Nicholas Festival in Demre/Kale.

9–17 December: Mevlana Festival at Konya. Hotels are packed for this, the only occasion in the year when the Whirling Dervishes can be seen performing.

December: Camel wrestling begins and continues throughout December and January in the province of Aydın, especially at Germencik.

TURKISH MUSIC AND DANCE

The lively Turkish folk music which originated on the steppes of Asia is in complete contrast to the refined Turkish classical music of the Ottoman court. Distinct also from the folk music is the Ottoman military music performed by the Janissary band in Istanbul, played with kettle drums, clarinets, cymbals and bells. Each region in Turkey has its own special folk dance and costume. In the Black Sea region for example is the 'Horon' dance, performed by men only, dressed in black with silver trimmings. The Sword and Shield Dance of Bursa represents the Ottoman conquest of the city, performed by men in early Ottoman battle dress. The well-known Spoon Dance is performed from Konya to Silifke by colourfully dressed men and women with a pair of wooden spoons in each hand.

Children

*T*urkey is a wonderful place for children as Turks love them and alway engage with them quite spontaneously. At mosque entrances they will help wit children's shoelaces and carry pushchairs up steps without needing to be asked.

Children love mosques. There is lots of space in the courtyard with ablution fountains to chase round, windows to peep out of and sills to climb upon. Best of all, there is no pressure to be sober and pious.

Most children will love a holiday in any of the Aegean and Mediterranean resorts, with good beaches and pedestrian town centres. Side is probably the most suitable of all. Eastern Turkey is less suitable as distances are large with long periods spent travelling. Turkish baths would not be enjoyed by children under five.

Child-related crime is unheard of in Turkey. The only negative safety factor is that rear seatbelts are a rarity, especially in taxis.

Babies

Pharmacies stock disposable nappies (though it is difficult to find the larger sizes, i.e. 12kg plus) along with tins of babies' powdered milk and packets of instant baby food that only need mixing with mineral water. Milupa is the commonest available brand. Baby food jars are not available. Johnson's baby products are available in all pharmacies as are Turkish equivalents of the usual children's medicines. Pharmacists usually speak English and are quite knowledgeable.

ISTANBUL

The whole of Istanbul is like one big playground, with mosques and palaces

and museums to frolic in and large areas of green space (see pages 42–3). Pushchairs can be a bit tricky as there are so many steps, in the nature of any city set on a hilly site. There is, however, always an obliging Turk to remove a turnstile or help navigate any apparent impasse at the crucial moment.

There are scores of actual playgrounds all over the city, notably along the European shore of the Golden Horn and round the Sea of Marmara shore. Slides are huge with 1 in 3 slopes and amazingly steep see-saws. Safety consciousness is not much in evidence in Turkey.

A permanent funfair with big wheel is set up on the shores of the Sea of Marmara on Kennedy Caddesi. At Ataköy, near the airport, there is Fame City, an amusements centre in the Galleria Shopping Mall.

The boat journeys up the Bosphorus or to Princes' Islands are fine, but with small children it is best to avoid the public steamers because of the scrum in getting on and off, and the dirt. These steamers are also totally unsuited to pushchairs. Children love the horse and carriage rides on Princes' Islands.

BEACHES

The best beaches for young children, with safe sandy bays, are at Alanya, Altınkum, Çeşme, Içmeler, Kemer, Ölü Deniz, Patara and Side. Avoid Kaş, Kalkan and the Black Sea beaches near Istanbul where there are dangerous undertows.

Selling water whistles at Pumukkale

CAVES

At Burdur the Insuyu Caves are directly on the main road north from Antalya, a good journey breaker. They have an extensive series of interlinked caves with underwater lakes and stalactites. Also near Antalya, 30km to the northwest, are the Karain Caves. At Alanya under the promontory rock are the Damlataş Caves with stalactites.

ZOOS

Antalya has a little zoo in the clifftop Karaalı Park. Istanbul has a small zoo in the Gülhane Park below the Topkapı Palace.

Sport

BALLOONING
Ninety-minute flights over the lunar landscapes of Cappadocia, daily, early in the morning, with champagne on landing included. Children under 12 are free. Cloud 9 SARL Professional Ballooning Services, Kapadokya Robinson Lodge, PO Box 48, 50200 Nevşehir, Türkiye.

CYCLING
Organised cycle tours are available in Cappadocia, a terrain well suited to bicycles with its relatively gentle gradients. It is an excellent way to appreciate the weird fairy chimney landscapes in leisurely fashion. The tours involve visits to some of the remoter churches and valleys, with fair amounts of walking required where terrain is not cyclable. Bicycle tours are also offered at Bodrum, Kuşadası, Marmaris and Turgutreis.
Cappadocia Tourbike, Istiklal Caddesi 10, Ürgüp (tel: 4861 34 88), have mountain bikes for hire.

FOOTBALL
The national sport played everywhere.

HORSERIDING
Cappadocia is the most popular region for this, and riding is an excellent way to explore the valleys full of rock-cut churches and cave dwellings. Short tours of less than a day can be arranged locally, but for longer holidays involving camping out, it is best to book an organised tour (usually about 10 people) from your own country. Your local tourist office will give you a list of specialist tour operators.

Horseriding is also available at Bodrum, Kuşadası, Ölü Deniz and Side.

MOUNTAINEERING
(See also pages 144-5.)
Specialist tour operators are:
Explore Worldwide, 1 Frederick Street, Aldershot, Hampshire GU11 1LQ, UK
Exodus, 9 Wier Road, London SW12 0LT, UK (081-675 5550).
Adventure Center, 5540 College Avenue, Oakland, California CA94618 (tel: 415-654 1879).
Mountain Travel Inc, 1398 Solano Avenue, Albany, California CA94706.

RAFTING
This sport is still in its infancy in Turkey, but can be practised in the Black Sea region on the Berhal, Berta, Çoruh, Fırtına, Hurşıt and Oltu rivers, and in the Mediterranean region the Cehennem stream and the Dragon, Göksu, Köprüçay and Manavgat rivers are suitable. Sobek Expeditions, PO Box 1089, Angels Camp, AC95222, USA (tel:209-736 4524), offers two-week trips down the Çoruh river from Baybur to Artvin.

SKIING
Uludağ, 34km from Bursa, is Turkey's premier ski resort at 1,900m with slopes for beginners and intermediates and a cluster of expensive hotels and restaurants. There are 25–30 pisted runs and lots of off piste, six chair-lifts and six T-bar lifts. Lifts are open 9am–dusk and the season is from December to the end of April. The village also has a heated swimming pool, an ice rink, a gym, discos and shops. There is a medical centre and ski school and ski equipment can be hired. Pistes are deserted mid-week, but get busier at

weekends. The standard of hotels is high.

Skiing at small resorts is also available at Erciyes Dağ, behind Kayseri, at Ilgaz Dağı and Elmadağ near Ankara, at Köroglu near Bolu, at Palandöken 4km south of Erzurum, at Sarıkamiş near Kars, and at Saklıkent near Antalya.

Specialist tour operators are:

Avia Tourism, Premier House, 77 Oxford Street, London W1R 7RB, UK (tel: 071-287 1378).

President Holidays, 542 Kingsland Road, London E8 4AH, UK (tel: 071-249 4002).

Simply Turkey, 8 Chiswick Terrace, Acton Lane, London W4 5LY, UK (tel: 081-673 7219).

TENNIS

Tennis courts are available in the resorts of Antalya, Bodrum, Fethiye, Gümbet, İçmeler, Kemer, Kuşadası, Ölü Deniz, Marmaris and Side.

WATERSPORTS

Watersports are on the increase all along the Aegean and Mediterranean coasts.

Alanya offers banana riding, paragliding, surfboards, waterskiing, windsurfing.

Altınkum offers jetskis, waterskiing, windsurfing.

Bodrum offers jetskis, parascending, scuba diving, windsurfing.

Fethiye offers dinghy sailing and windsurfing.

Gümbet offers parascending, pedaloes, jetskis, sailing, waterskiing and windsurfing.

İçmeler offers jetskis, pedaloes, scuba diving, waterskiing and windsurfing.

Kemer offers pedaloes, sailing, waterskiing and windsurfing.

Kuşadası offers paragliding, jetskis, scuba diving, waterskiing and windsurfing.

Ölü Deniz offers banana riding,

Paragliding at Fethiye

paragliding, pedaloes, waterskiing and windsurfing.

Marmaris offers pedaloes, scuba diving, windsurfing.

Side offers paragliding, pedaloes, waterskiing, windsurfing.

Turunç Bay offers banana riding, scuba diving, waterskiing, windsurfing.

Scuba Diving

At Fethiye and at Turunç Bay there are professional diving centres catering for beginners and advanced divers. A five-day course leads to an internationally recognised diving certificate.

Yachting

There are fully equipped yachting marinas at (starting in the North Aegean and moving southwards), Istanbul, Çanakkale, Çeşme, Siğacık, Kuşadası, Bodrum, Datça, Marmaris, Göçek, Fethiye, Kalkan, Kaş, Finike, Kemer, and Antalya. Foreign flagged yachts are allowed to sail in or between Turkish ports free of charge provided the yacht owner is on board.

Istanbul Sailing Club, Fenerbahçe (tel: 336 06 33).

Food and Drink

*T*urkish cuisine ranks with French and Chinese as one of the great cuisine of the world. Eating out is a national pastime that Turks take seriously an derive great pleasure from at the same time. Because of this, there is an end less variety of eating places on offer, all very good value, and since Turke grows all its own produce the quality and freshness is excellent.

There are several types of eating place to be aware of:

Kahve: a coffee house, usually men only, serving coffee and tea.

Lokanta: an informal restaurant serving home-cooked Turkish meals with non-alcoholic drinks.

İçkili lokanta: as above but licensed for alcohol.

Gazino: as above plus entertainment.

Kebapçi: serving various Turkish grilled meats.

Pideci: Turkish pizza parlour.

Restoran: a more formal restaurant serving international as well as Turkish dishes, with alcohol.

Turkish Delight with pistachio

In eating places where food is displayed, choose from the display rather than the menu. In *lokantas* there is often no menu, and you go to the kitchen to choose.

In restaurants a 10 or 15 per cent service charge is normally added to your bill, but it is usual to leave an extra 5 per cent for the waiter. In *lokantas* no service is added, so leave 10 per cent.

Istanbul, as ever, offers the biggest range and best-quality eating places in the country, with some extremely sophisticated restaurants, many with Bosphorus views. Prices for a meal without alcohol range from cheap in the simple *lokantas* to expensive in the top places. As you travel eastwards, the food and eating places become less good and less varied, but prices drop accordingly.

Starting with Istanbul, the following restaurant listings are grouped by region and are placed in four price brackets, indicating cost per person without alcohol:

T	cheap
TT	moderate
TTT	bit pricey
TTTT	very expensive

ISTANBUL

FISH

Kumkapı, the lively fishermen's quarter just 2km west of the Blue Mosque, is

Seemingly all the fish in the sea on display to attract the buyer to this Istanbul fish shop

where most Turks go for fish and *rakı*, with over 70 small, reasonably priced restaurants crammed into the narrow streets. Many have belly dancers too. The best known fish restaurants on the Bosphorus are at Sarıyer, Tarabya and at Anadolu Kavağı, and these tend to be more expensive.

Ali Baba TT
Good fish and *meze* in a garden beside the Bosphorus. *Open: noon–midnight. Kireçburnu Caddesi 20, Kireçburnu (tel: 262 08 89).*

Deniz Park Gazinosu TT
Well-established *lokanta* run by a Greek family. On the Bosphorus with fabulous views from the terrace. *Open: noon–11pm. Daire Sokak 9, Yeniköy (tel: 262 04 15).*

Façyo TTTT
The best in Tarabya, an area famous for

its nightlife and Bosphorus restaurants. Reservations essential. *Open: noon–midnight. Kireçburnu Caddesi 13, Tarabya (tel: 262 00 24).*

Huzur (Arabın Yeri) TT
Long established with a spectacular view of Europe at sunset. Reserve a window seat. *Open: noon–midnight. Salacak Iskelesi 20, Üsküdar (tel: 333 31 57).*

Körfez TTT
Beautiful top-class restaurant on the Asian side of the Bosphorus with a lovely summer terrace and its own boat to take you across from Rumeli Hisar. *Open: noon–3pm and 8pm–12pm. Körfez Caddesi 78, Kanlıca (tel: 332 01 08).*

Urcan TTT
Casual restaurant serving fish chosen from a tank, among the best in Istanbul. *Open: noon–midnight. Orta Çeşme Caddesi 2/1, Sarıyer (tel: 242 03 67).*

INTERNATIONAL

Baca TTT

Bar and restaurant with terrace affording
spectacular view of Bosphorus Bridge.
Be prepared for the steep steps to climb
to entrance. Live music and disco. *Open:
8pm–4am. Emirgan Yolu 58, Boyacıköy
(tel: 277 08 08).*

Bilsak TT

Restaurant, café and bar with French
cuisine and views of Maiden's Tower.
Live jazz. *Open: noon to midnight. Meclisi
Mebusan Caddesi 22, Fındıklı (tel: 252 38
68).*

Café Amadeus/Schnitzel Unlimited
TT

Viennese patisserie also serving good-
value schnitzel and salad with rustic
decor. *Open: 11am–11pm. Closed
Mondays. Köybaşı Caddesi 57-59,
Yeniköy (tel: 262 06 35).*

Le Chalet TTT

Chic restaurant with French cuisine by
candlelight overlooking the Bosphorus.
Some tables in the garden. *Open:
noon–midnight. Postacı Halil Sokak 280/3,
Tarabya (tel: 262 33 15).*

Tiendes TTT

Charming place for outdoor dining
beside the Bosphorus. Live music. *Open:
from 5pm. Muallim Naci Caddesi 149,
Kuruçeşme (tel: 263 02 23).*

ITALIAN

Little Italy TT

In an old apartment building in Beyoğlu
with painted ceilings. *Open:
noon–11.30pm. Istiklal Caddesi 251-253,
1st floor, Beyoğlu (tel: 243 17 18).*

Pizza Papillon TT

Oldest pizza place in the city with 15
different varieties. *Open: noon–11pm.
Selçuklar Sokak, Beşinci Yıl Çarşışı 21/3,
Etiler (tel: 257 39 46).*

KEBAB AND MEAT

Sultanahmet Köftecisi T

Good, old, modest *lokanta* popular for
its *köfte* meatballs. *Close to Ayasofya
Meydanı. Divanyolu Caddesi 28,
Sultanahmet (tel: 526 27 82).*

Yeni Çeşni TT

New Turkish meat restaurant with
garden and small pool. *Open: 9am–1am.
On the Asian side. Mahur Sokak,
Çiftehavuzlar (tel: 360 38 60).*

ORIENTAL

The Chinese Restaurant TT

Istanbul's first, opened in 1958, and still
very good. *Open: noon–3pm and
7pm–11pm. Lamartin Caddesi 17/1,
Taksim (tel: 250 62 63).*

RUSSIAN

Süreyya TTT

Gastronomic landmark of the city,
founded by a Russian émigré.
Reservation essential. *Open: noon–3pm
and 8pm–12.30am. Istinye Caddesi 26,
Istinye (tel: 277 58 86).*

TURKISH

Abdullah Efendi TTT

Set in a beautiful garden on a hill
overlooking the Bosphorus, a large,
long-established restaurant. *Open:
noon–3pm and 7pm–midnight. Koru
Caddesi 11, Emirgan (tel: 277 57 21).*

sitane TTT
ovely setting in restored Ottoman
ouse.Kariye Museum near by. *Open:
oon–3pm and 7.30pm–11.30pm. Kariye
otel, Kariye Camii Sokak 18, Edirnekapı
el: 534 84 14).*

içek Pasajı T
ollection of small restaurants serving
eze and meat dishes in a former flower
arket. No credit cards. *Istiklal Caddesi,
alatasaray, Beyoğlu.*

Darüzziyafe TT
uthentic Ottoman cuisine. Courtyard.
*Open: noon–3.30pm and 6pm–midnight.
Darüşşifa Sokak, Beyazıt (tel: 511 84 14).*

Galata Tower TTT
ig tourist attraction with live music and
elly dancing. Reservation essential.
*Open: noon–3pm and 8pm–midnight.
Kuledibi (tel: 245 11 60).*

**The Khedive's Summer Palace
(Hıdiv Kasrı)** TT
n a fine restored 19th-century palace on
ne Asian side. Live music. *Çubuklu (tel:
31 26 51).*

Konyalı TT
Within the Topkapı Palace, with lovely
Bosphorus views. *Topkapı Sarayı,
ultanahmet (tel: 513 96 97).*

.iman TT
Beside the harbour with lovely view.
*Open: noon–4pm only. Closed weekends.
Yeni Yolcu Salonu Üstü, Karaköy (tel: 244
0 33).*

**Memduh Pasa Yalısı/Günay
Restaurant** TTT
n a beautiful Ottoman *yalı* (summer-
ouse) on the Bosphorus. Pretty garden.

*Open: 8pm–midnight. Tarabya Caddesi
4/6, Kireçburnu (tel: 262 20 17).*

Pandeli TT
Famous landmark above the Egyptian
Spice Bazaar, with tiled alcoves. *Open for
lunch only. Closed Sundays. Mısır Çarşışı,
Eminönü (tel: 527 39 09).*

Refik T
Modest *lokanta* with Black Sea dishes.
*Open: noon–midnight. Sofyalı Sokak 10-
12, Tünel (tel: 243 28 34).*

Sarnıç TTT
Former Roman cistern. Curiosity value.
*Open: noon–3pm and 8pm–midnight.
Sogukçeşme Sokak, Sultanahmet (tel: 512
42 91).*

Subaşı T
Simple *lokanta*. Always good food.
Crowded. *Nuruosmaniye Caddesi,
Cagaloglu.*

Hot chestnuts for sale

Pandeli's Restaurant, above the Egyptian Spice Bazaar, Istanbul

TURKISH CUISINE

The most exciting thing in Turkish food
is the *meze*, the delicious range of little
appetisers which can either be a meal in
themselves or the forerunner to the main
course. It is in these *meze* that Turkish
cooks use their imagination and creativity
to dream up, for instance, 101 things to
do with an aubergine. They are excellent
for vegetarians as they consist of such
items as *börek* (small pastry cases filled
with cheese and herbs), *dolma* (vine
leaves stuffed with rice), aubergine dips
and salads, yogurt and garlic dips. Olive
oil is a key ingredient in all Turkish food,
and some may find the food too oily.
Others swear by it and are convinced it is
the secret of the lush hair growth enjoyed
in all Mediterranean countries. Great
care is taken with presentation and each
little dish will be garnished with parsley,
lemon or olives. Freshly baked Turkish
bread (*pide*) is supplied with *meze* in
limitless quantities.

With four seas washing the
shorelines, fish is another key ingredient,
with treated fish titbits like *hamsi*
(anchovies) forming part of a *meze*,
while for main courses there is sea bass,
bonito, swordfish, squid, giant prawns,
red bream, striped bream, gurnard and
striped goatfish. Fish is generally more
expensive than meat, unless you seek
out some of the *lokantas* in Kumkapı.
Riverfish, as at Bafa, Eğridir, Iznik and
Manavgat is particularly good value and
is always fresh.

Lamb is the most popular meat, used
in the well-known *şiş kebab* and *döner
kebab*, but also made into spiced meat
balls (*köfte*). Chicken is used less often,
but is very tasty when prepared with
walnuts, garlic and paprika as in
Circassian chicken.

The accompaniments to main
courses are usually rice (*pilav*) –
sometimes served with pine nuts,
currants and spices – and salads.

Desserts apart from fresh fruit and ice cream tend to be extremely sweet, as in delicate milk puddings scented with rosewater or honey-soaked pastries garnished with nuts, with names like Lady's Navel, Nightingale's Nest and Minister's Finger.

A sample Turkish menu in a good restaurant might read as follows:

Mezeler (Hors d'oeuvres)
Arnavut ciğeri: spicy fried liver with onions
Çerkes tavuğu: cold chicken in walnut purée with garlic
Çiğ köfte: spicy raw meatballs
Midye dolması: stuffed mussels
Yaprak dolması: stuffed vine leaves

Çorbalar (Soups)
Yala çorbası: yogurt soup
Düğün çorbası: meat soup with egg yolks stirred in
İkembe çorbası: tripe soup

İzgaralar (Grilled meats)
Bonfile: fillet steak
Döner kebab: lamb grilled on a revolving spit
Pirzola: lamb chops
Şış kebab: grilled lamb on skewers
İskender kebab: lamb pieces in tomato and yogurt sauce
Şış köfte: grilled meatballs

Pilavlar (Rices)
Sade pilav: plain rice pilaf
İç pilav: rice with pine nuts, currants and onions
Bulgur pilavı: cracked wheat pilaf

Zeytinyağlılar (Cold vegetables in olive oil)
İmam bayıldı: split aubergine with tomatoes and onions
Kabak kızartması: fried baby marrow slices with yogart
Patlıcan kızartması: fried aubergine slices with yogurt
Zeytinyağlı fasulye: green beans in tomato sauce

Börekler (Savoury pastries)
Sigara börek: fried filo pastry filled with cheese
Talaş böregi: puff pastry filled with meat

Salatalar (Salads)
Cacık: chopped cucumber in yogurt with garlic
Çoban salata: mixed tomato, pepper, cucumber and onion
Patlıcan salatası: puréed aubergine salad
Piyaz: haricot bean salad

Tatlılar (Desserts)
Baklava: flaky pastry stuffed with nuts in honey syrup
Tel kadayıf: shredded wheat stuffed with nuts in syrup
Sütlaç: creamy cold rice pudding
Komposto: cold stewed fruit
Dondurma: ice cream
Meyvalar: fruits

The standard Turkish breakfast consists of freshly baked bread, white goat's cheese, black olives, tomatoes, yogurt, honey and jam, with sweet black tea.

For snacks, there are kiosks in all cities selling things like *lahmacun*, thin pizza with mincemeat on top, rolled up and eaten like an ice-cream cone, or *köfte* and salad stuffed into pitta bread. These days Turkey caters for the pizza and chips fans as well, and in some of the Aegean resorts like Bodrum and Marmaris, you can even eat Chinese and Thai.

ISTANBUL ENVIRONS

BURSA
Anadolu Evi TT is in an old house above Tophane Park with superb views over the town.
Hünkar Doner Kebab House TT is the best of the bunch beside the Yeşil Cami, giving on to the peaceful cobbled square between Yeşil Cami and Yeşil Türbe.

There is also a fine selection of restaurants in the Kültürpark.

BÜYÜK ADA
Many fish restaurants line the promenade, with simple kebab restaurants in the little town square.

IZNIK
The lakeside fish restaurants make a good lunch stop.

AEGEAN REGION

APHRODISIAS
Near the village of Dandalaz, 3km before the site, there are several attractive riverside restaurants serving freshly caught trout.

Baklava sprinkled with pistachio

BEHREMKALE
There is a small selection of restaurants on the waterfront.

BODRUM
Han Restaurant TT is one of the most attractive, in a converted 18th-century *caravanserai* with dancing in the central courtyard.

Lining the seafront and inland are myriad restaurants, ever changing, many of them specialising in fish.

ÇANAKKALE
There are many reasonably priced restaurants on the promenade.

DALYAN
There is a small selection of fish restaurants along the riverbank.

FOÇA
An attractive collection of restaurants, many of them for fish, along the harbourfront.

IZMIR
Park Restoran TTT
Set in the Kültürpark, offering international cuisine with French overtones. *Kültürpark İçi (tel: 89 35 90).*

1888 Restaurant TTT
Serving delicious Mediterranean food with Sephardic Jewish specialities. Live music at weekends. *Cumhuriyet Bulvarı 248, Alsancak (tel: 21 66 90).*

Deniz Restoran TT
Has unusual *meze* and delicious squid, on the harbourfront. *Atatürk Caddesi (Kordon) 188/B (tel: 22 06 01).*

Kemal'in Yeri TT
Offers friendly service and wonderful

sh. *1453 Sokak 20/A, Alsancak (tel: 22
1 90).*

obiki TTT
n interesting Japanese restaurant,
losed Sundays. *Cumhuriyet Bulvarı 236,
lsancak (tel: 63 04 24).*

1ask TTT
legant place with bar, dancing and
aternational cuisine. *1453 Sokak 18,
lsancak (tel: 63 04 25).*

ejetaryen Lokantası T
'or vegetarians. *1375 Sokak 11/1,
lsancak (tel: 21 75 58).*

USADASI
n endlessly changing variety all round
ae harbour and town.

ARMARIS
good selection of Turkish and fish
estaurants of all price ranges along the
romenade and in the backstreets of the
ld town.

URUNÇ BAY
Ian Restaurant T in front of Pension
Dede offers good cheap food.

MEDITERRANEAN REGION

ALANYA
good range of fish and Turkish
estaurants to be found all along the
aain road.

ANTALYA
.he best restaurants are concentrated
n the clifftop in the Karaalı Park on the
oad to Lara, with excellent sea views,
nd a few scattered around the old
aarina.

Cheese for sale

ASPENDOS
Belkis Restaurant TT 2km before the
site, serves fresh river trout with a
terrace on the water's edge.

FETHIYE
There is a good range of moderately
priced restaurants along the promenade
and in the narrow streets inland.

FINIKE
Petek Restaurant TT serves good
Turkish food.

KALKAN
Kalkan is renowned for its excellent
cuisine. Among the best are **Korsan**
TT, **Han** TT (set price), **Kalkan Han**
(maximum 15 people), **Lipsos** and
Oasis, all moderately priced.

KAŞ
Has a good range of small restaurants,
some chic, some homely.

KEMER
Offers a wide range of small restaurants
in its back streets.

ANKARA AND CENTRAL ANATOLIA REGION

ANKARA

Casa Bonita TT
A new Mexican restaurant with tequila. *Reşit Galip Caddesi, Gölgeli Sokak 17/A Gaziosmanpaşa (tel: 446 30 66).*

Chez Le Belge TT
On the shores of Gölbaşı lake, 20km south of the city, specialising in fresh crayfish. *Gölbaşı on the road to Konya (tel: 484 14 78).*

Iskele TT
Excellent fish restaurant. *Tuna Caddesi, Kızılay (tel: 433 38 13).*

Kale restaurant (Boyacızade Konağı) TTT
Turkish cuisine in a lovely old timbered house with classical Turkish music and good views over Ankara from the terrace. *Berrak Sokak 9, Anadolu Medeniyetleri Müzesi yanı (tel: 310 25 25).*

Mangal 2 TT
Turkish cuisine in a restored Ankara house. *Kuloglu Sokak 26, Çankaya (tel: 440 09 59).*

Merkez Lokantası TT
Good meat and kebab restaurant. *Çiftlik Caddesi 72 (tel: 213 17 50).*

Poupee Donen TTT
At the top of Atakule Tower, with an aerial view of Ankara. *Atakule (tel: 440 74 12).*

Wine House TT
Informal friendly atmosphere, with simple salad and cheese platters. *Boğaz Sokak 28, Kavaklıdere (tel: 467 65 25).*

Yunus's TTT
Italian and Turkish cuisine, with a vegetarian menu and live music. *Cemal Nadir Sokak 18, Çankaya (tel: 438 58 56*

CAPPADOCIA

ÜÇHISAR

Bindelli Restaurant TT
Offers set menus in a cave with chunky earthenware pottery. The distinctive loca wine should be sampled. *Next to the Kay Motel.*

SIVAS

Şadrıvan Restoran TT
Surprisingly classy. *Situated in the town centre.*

KONYA

Damla Restaurant TT *off Mevlana Caddesi.*

EASTERN REGION AND THE BLACK SEA COAST

In contrast to Istanbul and the Aegean and Mediterranean regions, where you are likely to get a far better meal in a restaurant than in a hotel, here it is the restaurants of the best hotels that also offer the best food in the most salubriou surroundings. Outside the hotels, there are very few restaurants of tourist class. Diyarbakır and Mardin are the culinary highpoints of eastern Turkey, with a heavy Arab influence in their cuisines. Along the Black Sea, the food improves little but is still not up to Aegean and Mediterranean standards. It is rare for restaurants outside hotels to serve alcohol.

ERZURUM

Güzelyurt Restaurant TT
Opposite Yakutiye Madrasa.

One of a good selection of harbour restaurants in Marmaris

MALATYA

Melita Restaurant TT

Much used by tour groups, next door to the Hotel Sinan. *Atatürk Caddesi (tel: 821 24300)*.

TRABZON

Trabzon Restaurant TT

On the main square opposite the Özgur Hotel.

TURKISH DRINK

Most people are surprised to discover that Turkey is the world's sixth largest wine producer. The word wine even originated from the Hittite language. Turkish wine (both red and white) is good. The best reds are Yakut, Buzbağ and Villa Doluca, and the best white is Çankaya. There is also the *rosé* Lâl, and the *primeur* Nevşehir. Also recommended is the Special Reserve Karmen and the semi-sweet Vadı.

Beer is the locally produced Efes, good and reasonably priced.

Rakı, an aniseed spirit, is the national alcoholic drink, usually mixed with ice and water, when it goes cloudy. Rakı goes well with *meze* and with fish, and Turks generally drink it as an accompaniment to food rather than by itself.

Ayran is the national non-alcoholic drink, a chilled unsweetened thin yogurt, an acquired taste, but very thirst-quenching and refreshing.

Turkish coffee (*kahve*) is drunk to finish a meal or at any time of day, served in tiny cups. You specify the sugar level: *sade*, no sugar; *az*, little sugar; *orta*, medium sugar; *çok şekerli*, lots of sugar.

Tea (*çay*) is drunk at any time, served black in little glasses on saucers with a tiny spoon for stirring in the sugar lumps.

Mineral waters are cheap and excellent and come both fizzy and still. Even locals drink them in preference to the tap water as they taste so much better.

The usual range of fizzy drinks like Coca Cola or fizzy lemonade (Sprite or Yedigün) are available. Street stalls also sell freshly squeezed juices like orange, carrot and apple.

Hotels and Accommodation

*T*he standard of accommodation in Turkey covers the full range from five star deluxe Hiltons and Sheratons in the cities right through to simple family run pensions in the towns and villages. At all levels standards are improvin year by year and most first-time visitors are pleasantly surprised by the high quality of the accommodation. This is not the Middle East with its malfunc tioning equipment and power cuts, but neither is it Europe with its immacu late plumbing and efficient chambermaids. Turkey falls somewhere i between. Service is invariably friendly and willing, and many of the newe hotels are imaginatively designed, following traditional styles. Standards o hygiene are on the whole high. Because of the Muslim custom of washin under running water, wash basins are rarely equipped with plugs. A privat toilet and shower for each room is the norm even in the smaller pensions.

The starred levels of hotel are as follows:

Five star equivalent: a luxury hotel with full facilities.

Four star equivalent: a very good hotel with above average facilities.

Three star equivalent: a good tourist hotel with a moderate level of comfort.

Two star equivalent: a simpler hotel with a moderate level of comfort, that may not have a dining room.

One star equivalent: a modest hotel o pension with simple facilities, usually offering just bed and breakfast and ofter with shared bathroom and toilet.

Five- and four-star hotels always have a TV and minibar in the rooms, as do many three-star hotels. Two-star and

The Istanbul Hilton Hotel

The Yesil Ev or 'Green House' Hotel near Ayasofya, Istanbul

below do not. Price fluctuations in the two and three star categories are considerable, often for no discernible reason.

The grading of hotels in Turkey is carried out by the Ministry of Culture and Tourism. It is however often confusing, and should not be compared to grading systems in other countries. The difference between what is classed a hotel as opposed to a motel, for example, is far from clear. Many good hotels choose not to be registered. All establishments registered with the Ministry of Culture and Tourism automatically add a 10 per cent tax to the bill. Some of the larger registered hotels also make half-board compulsory. Since it is frequently cheaper and more pleasant to eat out in a restaurant (except in eastern Turkey, where the hotel restaurant is your best bet anyway), it is worth establishing the position before you book.

Air-conditioning is welcome in the months of July and August, and most four-star hotels and upwards have it, along with a few three star hotels. In the coastal resorts hot water is generally achieved by solar heating (except in the very large hotels), so in the evenings you should be aware that supplies are finite and should be used sparingly. During the day you can use as much as you like, as it will all be replenished before sunset anyway. Pensions tend to have simpler rooms than hotels, less well furnished and often short on wardrobe and storage space. Shower rooms in pensions often have no curtain or tray, so are a fairly watery experience.

Coastal hotels and pensions get very booked up on national holidays and at the two major religious feasts (Feast of Ramadan and the Feast of Sacrifice), but inland, with the exception of major tourist attractions like Pamukkale, you can usually find pleasant and uncrowded accommodation at places like Lake Eğridir.

The lounge bar at the Pera Palas Hotel in Istanbul

ISTANBUL

The accommodation available in Istanbul falls into several distinct types. First there are the top range international hotels like the Hiltons and Sheratons which are virtually the same the world over. Then there are the older imperial style hotels like the Pera Palas, purpose-built in 1892 for Orient Express travellers, or the restored Ottoman palaces like the Çırağan-Kempinski, Istanbul's most lavishly decorated hotel. Then there are the middle range modern hotels like the Kalyon or the Etap. The most exciting and interesting category of hotel in Istanbul is the converted Ottoman house. The Turkish Touring and Automobile Club has in recent years bought up and renovated several groups of old wooden Ottoman houses, refurbishing them in traditional style with polished wood floors and rugs. If you want to stay within easy walking distance of the Ayasofya, Blue Mosque and Topkapı Palace, that is, in the heart of old Istanbul, then the best hotels are these restored Ottoman houses like the Yeşil Ev, the Aya Sofya and the Sumengen. If you want a sea view as well, try the Kalyon Hotel on the Marmara shore below the Blue Mosque.

ISTANBUL ENVIRONS

Bursa has good accommodation ranging from the five-star Kervanserai with its own thermal baths, to three-star hotels for the more budget conscious. Büyük Ada has a couple of good moderately priced hotels, and Edirne has a few simple hotels equating to two and three stars.

AEGEAN REGION

Izmir has a Hilton and other four-star hotels, while the resorts of Kuşadası, Ayvalık and Çeşme offer the biggest each hotels. Marmaris has several larger modern hotels as does nearby Turunç Bay, but also many smaller family-run places. Accommodation in Bodrum tends to be very attractive, all low-rise by law, in traditional-style chalets, often set round pools and gardens with cascades of flowers. The smaller resort of Altınkum has modern purpose-built hotels, but not as big as those of Kuşadası, while the simpler fishing villages of Dalyan and Foça offer attractively designed smaller hotels and pensions. At Pamukkale it is best to choose one of the hotels up on the high plateau near the ruins as these have their own hot pools. They get very full, so book well ahead unless you are out of season.

MEDITERRANEAN REGION

The cities of Antalya, Antakya, Adana and Mersin all have modern four-star hotels. Elsewhere, the mixture is as before: purpose-built resort hotels (sometimes with their own beaches, as at Kemer) and smaller, more individual family-run pensions.

ANKARA AND CENTRAL ANATOLIA

Ankara has a Hilton and Sheraton, and these top range hotels tend to be in Yenişehir (the new district). The more modest places are generally located in the older Ulus Meydanı area. Tokat boasts a new four-star hotel, and Amasya, Boğazkale and Konya all have good moderately priced two- to three-star hotels, while Sivas provides simpler, old-style hotels of one- and two-star rating. Cappadocia has the full range from larger four-star modern hotels to small character places like the Club Med's Kaya Motel, dug out of the cliff.

EASTERN TURKEY AND THE BLACK SEA COAST

Accommodation here is far more limited than in the rest of Turkey, and each large town or city tends to have just one or two good hotels (equating to two or three stars). If these should happen to be full, the distance between these and the next hotel is enormous, so it is advisable to book ahead if you are travelling between May and September. Diyarbakır, Doğubeyazıt, Erzincan, Erzurum, Tatvan, Urfa and Van all have good standard hotels, while in Elazığ and Kars the level equates rather to one- or two-star hotels. For Nemrut Dağı the best accommodation is at Kâhta, and there are even hotels close to the summit now.

Along the Black Sea, Samsun and Trabzon have the best hotels, equating to two or three stars, and the smaller resort towns like Hopa, Akçakoca, Amasra, Ordu, Giresun and Sinop all have simple smaller accommodation equating to one or two stars. Inland, Bolu and Safranbolu both have a number of three-star hotels.

Hotel in Istanbul's Hippodrome

On Business

ANKARA BUSINESS CENTRE
This offers the best all-round service for visiting business people, with facilities for short or long-term office rental, translation and interpreting, wordprocessing and secretarial skills, recruitment consultancy, telephone, fax, telex and photocopying, and travel. Ankara Business Centre, Simon Bolivar 10/4, Çankaya, Ankara (tel: 440 30 20 or fax: 440 30 24) and now also at Sheraton Ankara Hotel and Towers, Noktalı Sokak, Kavaklıdere (tel: 468 07 45/46 or fax: 468 04 55).

BANK ACCOUNTS
Foreigners may keep their foreign currency in a Foreign Exchange Deposit Account in any bank authorised to exchange foreign currency.

BRIBERY
Anyone found offering any sort of bribe, money or gifts, especially to a government employee, is liable to imprisonment.

BUSINESS HOURS
Banks
Monday to Friday, 8.30am–noon and 1.30pm–6pm.
Business offices
Monday to Friday, 8.30am–5.30pm or 9am–6pm.
Government offices
Monday to Friday, 8.30am–12.30pm and 1.30pm–5.30pm.

BUSINESS VISAS
As for tourist visas, with 90-day visas issued automatically at the point of entry.

CAPITAL INVESTMENT
Foreigners may invest foreign capital in Turkey as hard currency, tangible fixed assets (e.g. machinery, tools) or intangible fixed assets (e.g. patents, trademarks). Income generated from an business, in the form of sales revenues o dividends for example, may be reinvested. The minimum investment is currently £50,000.

CHAMBERS OF COMMERCE
Ankara Chamber of Commerce, *Şeh Teğmen Kalmaz Caddesi 30, Ankara (tel: 4-310 4145 or fax: 4-310 8436).*
The British Chamber of Commerce of Turkey, *Mesrutiyet Caddesi No 34, Tepebaşı, Istanbul (tel: 1-249 0658 or fax: 1-242 5551).*
Istanbul Chamber of Commerce, *PC Box 377, Eminönü, Istanbul (tel: 1-511 4150 (44 lines) or fax: 1-526 2197).*
Izmir Chamber of Commerce, *Atatürk Caddesi 126, Izmir (tel: 51-144355 or fax: 51-137853).*
There are also Chambers of Commerce at Adana, Balıkesir, Bursa, Denizli, Eskişehir, Gaziantep, Iskenderun, Izmit, Kayseri, Mersin and Samsun.

CONFERENCE FACILITIES
The **Marmara Istanbul Hotel** has the largest conference facilities in the city, at Taksim Square 80090, Istanbul (tel: 1-251 46 96 or fax: 1-244 05 09). Most four- and five-star hotels in all Turkey's cities offer conference facilities.

ETIQUETTE
It is very important in Turkey to establis a good personal relationship prior to a business relationship, allowing time for

riendly chat before embarking on
business topics.

EXCHANGE RATES
There is a free foreign exchange market.
Prices follow Central Bank exchange
quotations and are printed in the *Turkish
Daily News*.

EXHIBITION ORGANISERS
**Afeks Organizasyon Pazarlama ve
Ticaret**, *Selime Hatun Camii Sokak
1/10, Findikli, Istanbul (tel: 1-243 4220
r fax: 1-251 6159).*

TUYAP Tum Fuarcilik Yapim AS,
*Saglam Fikir Sokak No 19, 80300
Esentepe, Istanbul (tel: 1-267 6705 or fax:
-267 1851).*

mbat Fuarcilik AS, *Selamlik Caddesi
1/3, Kızılay, Ankara (tel: 4-417 0603 or
ax: 4-417 5253).*

deal Uluslararası Fuar, *Ahmet Mithat
Efendi Sokak 20/1, 06550 Çankaya,
Ankara (tel: 4-440 6661 or fax: 4-438
235).*

zfas Izmir Fuarancilik, *Hizmetleri
Kültür ve Sanat Etkinikleri Tic AS, Sair
Esref Bulcam 50, Kültürpark, Izmir (tel:
1-142150 or fax: 51-254342).*

FOREIGN CAPITAL
Any transactions related to the use of
foreign capital come under the
discretion of the State Planning
Organisation's Foreign Capital
Department. All foreigners wanting to
initiate business operations in Turkey
must first obtain permission from this
body.

LANGUAGE
Trade literature may be in English,
French or German, but it is essential
that technical catalogues or leaflets be in
Turkish.

LOCAL AGENTS
Most government business is centred on
Ankara and is conducted on the public
tender system. It is essential to have
competent local representation.

MARKET RESEARCH
The best company to conduct
independent market research in Turkey
is **IBS (Istanbul Business Services)**,
*Abdi Ipekci Caddesi No 59/4, Maçka
80200, Istanbul (tel: 1-231 0481 or fax:
1-231 6614).*

MEDIA
There is a weekly economics and
business publication called *Barometer*, in
Turkish, which offers advertising space.

PREMISES
Premises may be found through a real
estate agent. These are listed in the
newspapers. For Sale (*satılk*) or For
Rent (*kıralık*) notices are put up on
vacant buildings and apartments.

RESIDENCE PERMITS
Called a *kimlik*, this is required by
foreigners wanting to stay longer than
three months. The maximum duration
of a residence permit is two years.

TAX
Foreign individuals, diplomats and
officials working for agencies of foreign
countries are exempt from income tax.
Foreigners whose residence is in Turkey
or who live in Turkey for more than six
consecutive months must pay tax.

WORK PERMITS
These are required by foreigners
wishing to work in Turkey. Permission
is obtained from the security
authorities.

Practical Guide

ARRIVING

Visas are required by British and Irish
nationals, and South Africans. They can
be bought on entry and are valid for
three months. They cost £5, payable in
foreign currency, with no change given.
Visas are not required for visitors holding
either Australian, Canadian, New
Zealand or American passports.

By air

Istanbul
Atatürk Istanbul Airport, where most
international flights arrive, is the
country's busiest, located at Yeşilköy,
25km west of the city centre. A taxi to
the centre takes 30 minutes and is
reasonably priced. There are cheaper
Turkish Airlines buses every hour to
Şişhane in the centre, but they do not
stop *en route*. Onward flights to North
Cyprus (Ercan) depart from the
international terminal, while transit
flights to other cities within Turkey
depart from the domestic terminal.

Other cities
Ankara and Izmir are the other two main
airports receiving scheduled international
flights. Izmir airport (Adnan Menderes)
is 30km south of the city, and Ankara
(Esenboğa) is 28km north of the centre.
Dalaman and Antalya, both on the
Mediterranean coast, take charter flights

By sea

There are three ways to arrive in Turkey
by boat. First from Venice, Italy. Turkish
Maritime Lines (TML) operate
comfortable car ferries from April to
October running once a week to Izmir.
Second, from North Cyprus (see page
140). Third, from the Greek islands (see
page 140).

By rail

Rail travel via Europe is difficult at the
moment because of the Balkan situation.
The former direct sleepers from Munich
and Vienna have been discontinued. Rail
travellers can, however, still reach
Istanbul from Greece or Bulgaria.

By car

No special documents are required for visits of under three months. The car is entered on the driver's passport as imported goods and must be driven out again in time. For stays of over three months, contact the Turkish Touring and Automobile Club, Halaskargazi Caddesi 364, Şişli, Istanbul (tel: 90-1-2314631) to obtain a _Carnet de Passage_.

CAMPING

There are 39 campsites in the Istanbul and Marmara region, 35 in the Aegean, 27 in the Mediterranean and 15 in Central Anatolia (largely Cappadocia). East of Adana there are no campsites and along the Black Sea coast there is no campsite between Zonguldak and Hopa. The majority have a restaurant, cooking facilities, hot showers and electricity. Caravans can be hired from Anadolu Karavan, Çiragan Müvezzi Caddesi 9/1, Beşiktas, Istanbul (tel: 260 14 80 or fax: 260 14 66). In Turkey the camping

THOMAS COOK
Traveller's Tip

Thomas Cook Network offices offer airline ticket re-routing and revalidation free of charge to MasterCard holders and to those who have bought their travel tickets from Thomas Cook.

organisation is Türkiye Kamp ve Karavan Dernegi, Nenehatun Caddesi 96, Gaziosmanpaşa, Ankara (tel: 136 31 51).

CHILDREN

Turks are delighted to have children at their hotels, restaurants and shops. Like most other airlines, Turkish Airlines (THY) offer the standard IATA child reductions; 90 per cent for under-twos and 50 per cent for two to twelves.

Istanbul taxis

CLIMATE

The best time to visit is between May and October. The tourist season in the coastal regions runs from 1 April to 31 October. July and August can be too hot for exploring sites in the midday sun.

> **WEATHER CONVERSION CHART**
> 25.4mm = 1 inch
> °F = 1.8 × °C + 32

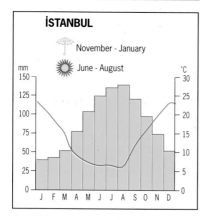

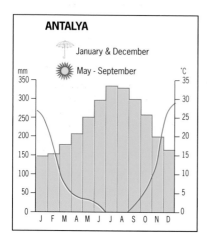

CRIME

Violent crime rates are low, as are petty crime rates, but it is always wise to take sensible precautions. In the event of a crime, report it to the Tourist Police (see later Police listing).

CUSTOMS REGULATIONS

On entry, dutyfree limits are 200 cigarettes and 50 cigars, 200 grams of tobacco, five 100cc or seven 70cc bottles of wine and/or spirits, five bottles of perfume, 120ml maximum each. The import of all narcotics is forbidden and carries stiff prison sentences. The export of antiquities is forbidden. Proof of purchase is required for a new carpet, and a certificate detailing age from a museum directorate for an old carpet.

DISABLED TRAVELLERS

Facilities are improving. Istanbul international airport now has adapted lifts and toilets, and ramps have been installed in some museums and in the state theatres, opera and concert halls. Turkish State Railways (TCDD) make a reduction of 70 per cent for disabled travellers, with a 30 per cent reduction for those accompanying them. For information: Özürluler Federesyonu, Gurabba Huseyinama Caddesi, Cineirraklibostan Sokak, Mermer Iş Hanı, Aksaray, Istanbul (tel: 534 59 80).

DRIVING
Car hire

This is expensive. Drivers must be over 21 and have a valid driving licence from their own country. The only legally required insurance is third party, but it is advisable to take out the extra Collision Damage Waiver and Personal Accident insurance which all rental firms offer.

Emergency

In the event of breakdown, call the Turkish Touring and Automobile Club Istanbul head office tel: 131 46 31). In the event of an accident the police must be notified.

Insurance

Motorists driving their own cars should get a Green Card from their home insurer to extend cover to Turkey.

Petrol

The available types are super (four-star), normal (two-star), unleaded (only in cities and still quite rare), and diesel. There are lots of petrol stations all over the country.

Roads

Turkey has a good, well-maintained road network. Turkish road signs conform to the international protocol. Traffic drives on the right and the Turkish highway code is similar to the European.

Speed limits

In towns the speed limit is 50kph and on state highways it is 90kph and on motorways 120kph.

ELECTRICITY

220 volts, 50 cycles and two-pin European plugs.

EMBASSIES AND CONSULATES

Australia: Ankara, Gaziosmanpaşa, Nenehatun Caddesi No 83 (tel: 4361240/43); Istanbul, Etiler, Tepecik Yolu Uzeri No 58 (tel: 2577050).
Canada: Ankara, Gaziosmanpaşa, Nenehatun Caddesi No 75 (tel: 4361275/79); Istanbul, Gayrettepe, Büyükdere Caddesi No 107, Bengün

Han, Kat 3 (tel: 2725174).
Ireland: Istanbul (Honorary Consul), Harbiye (tel: 246 60 25).
United States of America: Ankara, Kavaklıdere, Atatürk Bulvarı No 110 (tel: 4265470); Istanbul, Tepebaşı, Mesrutiyet Caddesi No 104/108 (tel: 251 36 02); Izmir, Alsancak, Atatürk Caddesi No 92 (tel: 849426).
United Kingdom: Ankara, Çankaya, Şehit Ersan Caddesi No 46/A (tel: 4274310/15); Istanbul, Beyoğlu/ Tepebaşı, Mesrutiyet Caddesi No 34 (tel: 244 75 40); Izmir, 1442 Sokak No 49, P.K.300 (tel: 211795); Antalya, Kazım Özalp Caddesi No 149/A (tel: 111851).

EMERGENCY TELEPHONE NUMBERS

Ambulance 112
Police 155
Fire 110
In Istanbul there are also private ambulance firms.
Thomas Cook travellers' cheque refund number, in case of loss or theft: 99 800 44 4895 (24-hour, toll-free).

THOMAS COOK
Traveller's Tip

Free emergency assistance is given at any Thomas Cook Network office. Ekin Turizm is the Network member for Thomas Cook in Turkey, with offices at Istanbul, Cumhuriyet Caddesi 295 and Ankara, Kızılırmak Caddesi, Mis Apt No 1, Akay. They will provide assistance in the event of loss or theft of Thomas Cook MasterCard Travellers' cheques or MasterCards.

LANGUAGE

Turkish is a UralAltaic language, related to Finnish and Hungarian, that has been written in Latin script since 1928 when Atatürk abolished the Arabic script used by the Ottomans.

Pronunciation

c = j as in cami (mosque) = jami
ç = ch as in Foça = Focha
ğ = soft g, unpronounced, it extends the preceding vowel as in dağ (mountain) = daa
ı (dotless i) = as in the initial a in away. For example, Topkapı = Topkapeu
ö = oe as in Göreme = Goereme
ş = sh as in Kuşadası = Kushadaseu
ü = as in French tu . For example, Ürgüp

Greetings and politenesses

Hello	*merhaba*
Goodbye	*güle güle* (said by the one staying behind) *allahaısmarladık* (said by the one leaving)
Good morning	*günaydın*
Good evening	*iyi akşamlar*
Good night	*iyi geceler*
Please	*lütfen*
Thank you	*mersi* or *teşekkur ederim*

Everyday expressions

Yes	*evet*
No	*hayır* or *yok*
There is	*var*
There is not	*yok*
I want	*istiyorum*
How much?	*ne kadar?*
Expensive	*pahali*
Cheap	*ucuz*
Money	*para*
Very beautiful	*çok güzel*
Toilet	*tuvalet*
Men's (toilet)	*baylar*
Women's (toilet)	*bayanlar*

Time

Today	*bugün*
Yesterday	*dün*
Tomorrow	*yarın*
What is the time?	*saat kaç?*

The days of the week

Sunday	*Pazar*
Monday	*Pazartesi*
Tuesday	*Salı*
Wednesday	*Çarşamba*
Thursday	*Perşembe*
Friday	*Cuma*
Saturday	*Cumartesi*

Numbers

1	*bir*	8	*sekiz*
2	*iki*	9	*dokuz*
3	*üç*	10	*on*
4	*dört*	20	*yirmi*
5	*beş*	50	*elli*
6	*altı*	100	*yuz*
7	*yedi*	1,000	*bin*

HEALTH

There are no mandatory vaccination requirements. Immunisation against typhoid, tetanus, polio and hepatitis A is recommended. There is no malaria risk in the Mediterranean coastal regions, but east of Ankara, anti-malarial tablets are recommended between March and November. Avoid swimming in fresh water near the Syrian border. AIDS is present in Turkey as in all parts of the world. Take sensible precautions over uncooked food, and drink only bottled water.

For minor problems go to the pharmacy (*eczane*) and describe your symptoms. If necessary, your hotel will call a doctor but there will be a charge for this. If hospital treatment is needed, use either the American Hospital in Nişantaşı, Istanbul (tel: 231 40 50), or the French Hospital behind the Divan Hotel, Taksim, Istanbul (tel: 148 47 56), or the German Hospital in Taksim, Istanbul (tel: 251 71 00). Treatment must be paid for, so medical insurance is essential.

On the coast, watch out for sea urchins whose black spines should not be trodden on, and jellyfish.

MEDIA

Turks are avid newspaper readers and there are a great many Turkish papers. The only English language daily is the *Turkish Daily News*. Foreign newspapers are available in the big cities one day late. The Voice of Turkey broadcasts in English from 7.30am–12.45pm and from 6.30pm–10pm on the following frequencies: 100.6Mhz, 97.4Mhz, 101.6Mhz, 100.5Mhz, 101.9Mhz and 103Mhz.

By taxi past Yeni Cami, Istanbul

Conversion Table

FROM	TO	MULTIPLY BY
Inches	Centimetres	2.54
Feet	Metres	0.3048
Yards	Metres	0.9144
Miles	Kilometres	1.6090
Acres	Hectares	0.4047
Gallons	Litres	4.5460
Ounces	Grams	28.35
Pounds	Grams	453.6
Pounds	Kilograms	0.4536
Tons	Tonnes	1.0160

To convert back, for example from Centimetres to inches, divide by the number in the the third column.

Men's Suits

UK	36	38	40	42	44	46	48
Rest of Europe	46	48	50	52	54	56	58
US	36	38	40	42	44	46	48

Dress Sizes

UK	8	10	12	14	16	18
France	36	38	40	42	44	46
Italy	38	40	42	44	46	48
Rest of Europe	34	36	38	40	42	44
US	6	8	10	12	14	16

Men's Shirts

UK	14	14.5	15	15.5	16	16.5	17
Rest of Europe	36	37	38 39/40	41		42	43
US	14	14.5	15	15.5	16	16.5	17

Men's Shoes

UK	7	7.5 8.5		9.5	10.5	11
Rest of Europe	41	42	43	44	45	46
US	8	8.5 9.5		10.5	11.5	12

Women's Shoes

UK	4.5	5	5.5	6	6.5	7
Rest of Europe	38	38	39	39	40	41
US	6	6.5	7	7.5	8	8.5

Struggling home with a new purchase

MONEY MATTERS

There is no limit on the amount of foreign currency that can be brought into the country, but no more than $5,000-worth of Turkish liras can be brought in or taken out. Keep your foreign exchange slips, you may have to show them when taking souvenirs out of the country to prove they have been purchased with legally exchanged money, or if you want to change any Turkish lira back to foreign currency. There are many banks and almost all will exchange foreign currency. Most three-star hotels and upwards offer an exchange service. Foreigners can use Visa cards to obtain local currency from cash dispensers at Iş Bank and Yapı-Kredi Bank (the latter also accepts Eurocard and MasterCard). Credit cards are widely accepted. Travellers' cheques and Eurocheques are easily exchanged in banks and at hotels. Thomas Cook MasterCard travellers' cheques can be quickly refunded in the event of loss or theft. Sterling and US dollar travellers' cheques are recommended. Except in the larger hotels, it is not usually possible to settle bills directly with travellers' cheques.

NATIONAL HOLIDAYS
Official Holidays

1 January	New Year's Day
23 April	National Sovereignty and Children's Day
19 May	Atatürk's Commemoration and Youth and Sports Day
30 August	Victory Day
29 October	Republic Day

Government offices and businesses shut on these days, but shops remain open.

Religious Holidays

There are two major Muslim festivals. The Feast of Ramadan, celebrating the end of the month of fasting, is a three-day national holiday. The Feast of the Sacrifice, celebrating Abraham's willingness to sacrifice his son Isaac, is a four-day national holiday. All hotels on the coast are full and all offices shut. The dates for these religious festivals follow the lunar calendar and therefore move backwards by 11 days each year.

OPENING HOURS

Banks: Monday to Friday, 8.30am–noon, 1.30pm–5pm.
Shops: Monday to Saturday, 9am–7pm.
Museums: 8.30am–noon and 1.30pm–5pm (winter) and 8.30am–5.30pm (summer). Closed Monday.
Government offices: Monday to Friday, 8.30am–12.30pm and 1.30pm–5.30pm.

ORGANISED TOURS

Most organised tours operate from Istanbul, with firms like Istanbul Vision Tour of Cumhuriyet Caddesi No 12/C, Elmadağ (tel: 241 3935; fax: 241 5764).

PHARMACIES

Pharmacists in Turkey are quite highly qualified, and can take your blood pressure or even give injections. Most non-addictive drugs and medicines can be bought without a prescription. Each district in large cities like Istanbul and Ankara has a pharmacy open 24 hours a day. The name of the duty pharmacy is listed in all the other pharmacies. Normal opening hours are Monday to Saturday, 9am–7pm.

PLACES OF WORSHIP

As well as the mosques for Muslim worship on most street corners, Istanbul has the Catholic San Antonio di Padova on Istiklal Caddesi, Beyoğlu, and the Anglican Saint Helena's Chapel at the British Consulate, Tepebaşı, and the Neve Shalom synagogue on Büyük Hendek Caddesi, Şişhane.

POLICE

Tourist Police are there to help tourists in the event of crime and are easily recognisable by their beige uniforms and maroon berets (Istanbul, tel: 527 45 03/528 53 69; Ankara: 134 17 56; and Izmir: 218 652/218 249). They also have offices in all towns throughout the country. Traffic police wear green uniforms and white caps, while Market police in blue uniforms patrol the markets and bazaars to check commercial practice. The Jandarmas (gendarmerie) are soldiers in green army uniform with a red armband who keep the peace, prevent smuggling, etc.

POST OFFICES

Turkish post offices are easily recognisable by their yellow PTT signs. In Istanbul and Ankara the main post offices are open 24 hours a day, while smaller ones throughout the country share government office hours. Poste restante letters should be addressed poste restante to the central post offices (*Merkez Postanesi*) in the town of your choice. Proof of identity is required on collecting poste restante.

Downtown Istanbul

PUBLIC TRANSPORT

Timetables and details of many trains, buses and ferries can be found in the Thomas Cook Overseas Timetable, published bi-monthly and obtainable from Thomas Cook branches.

Air

Turkish Airlines (THY) operates internal flights between Ankara, Istanbul, Izmir, Adana, Antalya, Dalaman, Diyarbakır, Erzurum, Gaziantep, Kayseri, Konya, Malatya, Trabzon and Van. THY has offices for ticket reservations in all major cities in the country. The main offices are: Istanbul (tel: 573 35 25 or fax: 240 29 89) and Ankara (tel: 312 49 00/309 04 00 or fax: 312 55 31).

Bus

This is the best way to get around in Turkey for smaller distances than require flying. The coaches are comfortable, air-conditioned, and the service is relatively inexpensive, efficient and reliable. Coaches/buses depart from bus stations, *otogar*, and seats should be booked a day or two in advance either at the local bus station or at a travel agent.

Train

Trains have first- and second-class seating, and some have restaurants and sleeping cars. On the European side, trains from Edirne and Greece arrive at Sirkeçi Station near Eminönü Square, while on the Asian side trains depart from Haydarpaşa Station (20 minutes across the Bosphorus by ferry) to Ankara and all points east. Tickets are bought at the station or reserved via a travel agent. Istanbul to Ankara takes 9 hours. The Mavi Tren (Blue Train) is the fast intercity service, leaving Haydarpaşa twice daily.

Taxi

Dolmuş taxis are the cheapest. These zippy minibuses run along specified routes and can be flagged down anywhere along the route. Dolmuş means stuffed, and they usually live up to their name. Normal taxis are metered and reasonable, the best way to travel in cities. They have a day tariff (one light on the meter) and a night tariff (two lights on the meter) when the rate is 50 per cent extra, chargeable only between 12pm and 6am.

Tram

Within Istanbul there are high-speed trams running from Aksaray to Ferhatpaşa and Sirkeçi. An old-fashioned tram still runs along Istiklal Caddesi between Galata and Taksim. If it suits your route, there is also the Tünel, the world's oldest and shortest subway, running from Karaköy up the hill to Beyoğlu.

Ferry

Turkish Maritime Lines (TML Central Office, Karaköy, Rıhtım Caddesi, Istanbul tel: 845 53 66/849 18 96 or fax: 851 57 67) run a car ferry from Istanbul to Izmir, Marmaris and Mersin, three times a week. TML also run a Black Sea line departing Mondays from Istanbul to Trabzon, calling at Sinop, Samsun, Ordu and Giresun, from May to October. Ferries from Istanbul and other ports across the Bosphorus are frequent and very cheap. Brass jetons are used as tickets, bought at the quayside. All Bosphorus ferries depart from the three quays beside the Galata Bridge.

STUDENT AND YOUTH TRAVEL

Holders of most internationally

recognised student cards are entitled to student reductions and accommodation at Turkish Youth Hostels. The main office is in Istanbul at Topkapı Atatürk Student Centre, Topkapı, Londra Asfaltı, Cevizlibag Duragı (tel: 582 20 455).

TELEPHONES

112	Emergency ambulance services
118	Directory enquiries and pharmacies on duty
131	Long distance operator
141	Telegrams by phone
161	Long distance enquiries
191	Long distance quick service operator
528-23-03	International operator

Cheap rates apply between 8pm and 8am.

Most three-star hotels and above have direct dial international lines from your room. The most economical way to telephone in Turkey is from a PTT booth. Jetons of three sizes for local, intercity and international calls, can be purchased from all PTT offices, as can telephone cards. To call abroad from Turkey dial 9 then, after a new tone, 9 again for an international line, then the country code, then the number itself. The UK country code is 44, Ireland is 353, USA is 1, Australia is 61, Canada is 1 and New Zealand is 64.

TIME

UK and Ireland are 2 hours behind Turkey all year round. Australia and New Zealand are 8 hours ahead while USA and Canada are 7 hours behind.

TIPPING

When 10–15 per cent service charge is added to your bill, it is customary to leave

Public phone boxes are yellow

an extra 5 per cent for the waiter. In smaller restaurants where service is not included, 10 per cent is normal. Taxi drivers do not expect tips. In a Turkish bath, the masseuses will be delighted with a TL5,000 to 10,000 tip. Mosque attendants can be given TL5,000 if they have opened something specially, while shoe attendants can be left TL1,000.

TOURIST OFFICES

Offices are all over the country and at the airports of Istanbul, Ankara, Izmir, Adana and Dalaman. At Istanbul there are additional tourist offices at the Hilton Hotel Arcade, Sultanahmet Square, Karaköy Maritime Station, and the Central Office at Mesrutiyet Caddesi 57/6, Beyoğlu (tel: 245 68 75 or fax: 243 65 64). They are open the same hours as government offices.

ACKNOWLEDGEMENTS

The Automobile Association wishes to thank the following organisations, libraries and photographers for their assistance in the preparation of this book:

J ALLAN CASH PHOTOLIBRARY 1, 67b, 88/9, 104b, 120, 123, 126, 130, 133, 135, 137, 149
DIANA DARKE 56, 79, 95, 128, 131, 139, 144
IMPACT PHOTOS (CAROLINE PENN) 138
KADIRLI TANITMA VE TURISM DERNEGI 105b
THE MANSELL COLLECTION LTD 66a, 67a
MARY EVANS PICTURE LIBRARY 20a, 46, 118a
NATURE PHOTOGRAPHERS LTD 148a (K J Carlson), 148b (P R Sterry)
GRANT PRITCHARD 161
REX FEATURES LTD 13
SPECTRUM COLOUR LIBRARY 7, 11b, 15b, 115, 118b, 125, 127, 129, 132, 141, 143, 145, 147, 158, 159
ZEFA PICTURE LIBRARY (UK) LTD Cover

The remaining photographs are held in the AA Photo Library and were taken by Dario Mitidieri, with the exception of the inset, spine and pages 9, 10, 11a, 11c, 14, 15a, 17, 18, 19a/b, 21a, 22, 23, 31a, 33, 39, 43, 44, 47a, 55, 74a, 75a/b, 150, 151, 152, 164, 167, 170, 171, 174, 176, 177, 184, 186, 189 which were taken by Antony Souter.

The Automobile Association would also like to thank the following people and companies for their help in the preparation of this book: Ms Ani Ablaoglu of Ekin Turizm, Istanbul; The Turkish Tourist Office, London

Series adviser: Melissa Shales

Copy editor: Dilys Jones